*Praise for*

## PARENTS UNDER THE INFLUENCE

"A worthy read for parents of children of all ages. Easy-to-assimilate lessons on creating a healthy and respectful relationship with your child."
— *Kirkus Reviews*

"This book is the beginning of a new oeuvre; not child psychology, more *parent psychology*. It is a beautifully wrought study of how children and parents relate, inspiring for its radical blend of the personally felt and the clinically observed."

—Isaac Mizrahi, designer, cabaret performer, talk-show host,
TV celebrity, and author of *I.M.*

"In her at once encyclopedic and utterly unpretentious, beautifully written book, *Parents Under the Influence*, Cécile David-Weill describes how and why we parent, and when and why we are most likely to make mistakes. She is neither academic nor proscriptive as she provides a passionate, deeply felt case for why parenting should be, at its best, a joy. Our one task as parents is to reckon with our own 'influence': *our* parents, *our* childhoods. As a mother, I am in awe of her ability to explode clichés and illuminate the essence of that most complex thing: raising another human being."

—Lea Carpenter, author of *Eleven Days*
and *Red, White, Blue*

ALSO BY CÉCILE DAVID-WEILL

*The Suitors*

# PARENTS
## UNDER THE
# INFLUENCE

## Words of Wisdom from a
## Former Bad Mother

### Cécile David-Weill

OTHER PRESS / NEW YORK

Chapter Two epigraph from *The Words* by Jean-Paul Sartre. English Translation
Copyright © 1964 by George Braziller. Originally published in France as *Les Mots*,
Copyright © 1964 by Éditions Gallimard. Reprinted by permission of Georges
Borchardt, Inc., for Éditions Gallimard. Chapter Eight epigraph from *The Notebooks
of Joseph Joubert*. Translation copyright © 1983, 2005 by Paul Auster. Published by
New York Review Books. All rights reserved. Chapter Nine epigraph from "La vie de
Famille" by Daniel Pennac and Robert Doisneau, © Éditions Hoëbeke

*Production editor: Yvonne E. Cárdenas*
*Text Designer: Jennifer Daddio / Bookmark Design & Media Inc.*
*This book was set in Goudy Old Style and Hypatia Sans*
*by Alpha Design & Composition of Pittsfield NH*

1 3 5 7 9 10 8 6 4 2

Library of Congress Cataloging-in-Publication Data

Names: David-Weill, Cécile, 1960- author.
Title: Parents under the influence : words of wisdom from a former bad mother /
Cécile David-Weill.
Description: New York : Other Press, 2020.
Identifiers: LCCN 2018056706 (print) | LCCN 2019006560 (ebook) |
ISBN 9781590510575 (ebook) | ISBN 9781590510568 (paperback)
Subjects: LCSH: Parenting. | Motherhood. | Self-actualization (Psychology) |
BISAC: FAMILY & RELATIONSHIPS / Parenting / Motherhood. | SELF-HELP /
Personal Growth / General. | BIOGRAPHY & AUTOBIOGRAPHY / Women.
Classification: LCC HQ755.8 (ebook) | LCC HQ755.8 .D368 2020 (print) |
DDC 306.874—dc23
LC record available at https://lccn.loc.gov/2018056706

TO MY PARENTS,

*who did what they could.*


TO MY CHILDREN,

*Pierre, Laure, and Alice,*

*For whom I did what I could,*

*And who inspired and supported me,*


AND TO THEIR CHILDREN

*Maya, Assya, Balthazar, Olivia, and Timur . . .*


*And to all those who have yet to be born.*

# Contents

# Preface

Who am I to say how we should raise our children?

To establish my authority in this matter, I might invoke the fact that I'm a mother, and now a grandmother as well. And this alone could very well be justification enough for me to talk about parenting. Casually, I could add that I am French and American, and also partly raised my children in Asia, which gives me a rather unique frame of reference. But above all, my ideas on the subject come from an even deeper and more personal experience, namely, that I am a former bad mother who nearly missed out on the joys of being a parent and on raising my children well. In other words, my perspective on how we should raise our children comes from the mistakes I made—mistakes I have since recognized and carefully attempted to correct.

It came as a total shock to me when I realized, fourteen years into parenthood, that my children didn't seem to be happy and thriving. Where had I been going wrong? What was wrong with me? I had always thought I would be a great

mom and had been doing my best to live up to that ideal.
But my decision to rely on a combination of love and instinct, hoping that this would be enough to overcome my
struggles as a mother, wasn't working for me or for them.
Half the time I would say to myself, "I'm terrible at this, but
I don't care," affecting a blithe indifference that in no way
corresponded to how I actually felt. The rest of the time I
would feel guilty when comparing my behavior with other
parents around me. In short, I was too caught up in myself
to really take an interest in my children and create bonds
with them.

Then I realized that it was not I who was doing the
parenting—my emotions were. Complicated feelings left
over from my childhood were confusing me, influencing
me, and often contradicting my conscious intentions as a
parent. I was "under the influence" of my childhood. And
this baggage was undermining my decisions and behavior
as a mother, preventing me from sticking to the parenting
philosophy I had hoped to follow.

Since the parenting guidebooks I'd avidly read, as good
as they may have been, never really raised this fundamental
question of the influence of my own emotional and famil-
ial history on my parenting, I came to the distressing conclusion that successful parenting was an impossibility and
that no reasonable human being could claim to do it well.
I felt this all the more when I realized, to my horror, that
unresolved emotions stemming from my childhood had
been driving me to actually *reproduce* my own upbringing,
including the behavior that had hurt me the most. As a result, regardless of all my good intentions and the incredible

energy I had devoted to motherhood, the way I interacted with my children often lacked judgment or reason and so didn't produce the intended results.

Of course, the notion of the unconscious mind wasn't new to me. But even though I didn't deny its influence on other aspects of my life, I never thought of how it might have an impact on how I raised my children. Is it because the very idea of the unconscious seems so irreconcilable with the maturity and discernment required to be a parent that acknowledging its influence on our parenting abilities is deeply unsettling? In any case, as a worried mother seeking reassurance, I had entirely avoided the question of the unconscious effects my own upbringing was having on the one I was trying to give my children.

Yet it only takes a minute's reflection to understand that it would be unreasonable to overlook this part of ourselves that keeps us from being consistent in our own parenting practices and, worse still, leads us unintentionally to harm our children. Over time I came to realize that I couldn't raise my children successfully without coming to terms with my own childhood.

It took me fifteen years of research, reflection, and practice to understand where my problems lay and how to overcome them. I had to take real steps to turn around my relationship with my children. And the profound transformation that ensued allowed them to develop into who they are today: three individuals I would love to meet even if I weren't their mother. I am so grateful for all I experienced and for how much I was able to change, and for who my children have become.

This journey has taught me that it is possible for us parents to let go of our childhoods and our pasts. It has also shown me that much of the work required to address how our own unresolved emotions may be affecting our parenting can be practiced daily while we interact with our children. The whole point of this book is to share the lessons I learned in the long process of changing my parenting.

I have to admit that I was initially hesitant to write this book. Because I am a novelist, I knew I could not offer a scholarly overview of parenting theories. I don't know enough about the history of these ideas to retrace them exhaustively or academically from their sources, nor am I able to explain how they have evolved and changed from one theorist or therapist to the next.

But I saw that I could write a book that grew out of painful but important personal experiences and insights. So I took a leap of faith, hoping that this approach might help other parents also "under the influence."

The result is a book I wish I'd had when I began raising my children: an empirical guide to parenting, supplementing my own experiences with concrete examples drawn from friends and acquaintances, as well as from case studies by therapists who trusted me with delicate information, and from works of fiction and pop cultural phenomena relating to the topic of parenthood. I have protected the privacy of those individuals who shared their stories with me by changing their names, and I have likewise protected my own children and their lives—a choice I'm sure many fellow parents can understand.

This book is aimed at all parents who find themselves under the influence—as I myself was, and sometimes still am. Indeed, I believe we are all under the influence when we don't acknowledge the impact our childhood has on our parenting style, and when we haven't developed the habit of questioning ourselves and setting constructive priorities for our children. My hope is that this book will help parents reflect upon their own unconscious assumptions and enable them to do the right thing for their children. After all, our parenting sets a template that, for better or for worse, stays with them for the rest of their lives.

# PART ONE

# THE INVISIBLE CONNECTION BETWEEN PARENTS AND CHILDREN

# 1

❧

# Children Draw
# on Our Behavior

*For children are either a blessing or a curse
according as they turn out;
and they turn out according as they are brought up.*

—MARIA EDGEWORTH, "The Contrast"
(in *Popular Tales*, 1817)

*Just as each person wishes his son to be,
so he turns out.*

—TERENCE, *Adelphoe*
("The Brothers"), 160 BCE

The qualities I thought made me most prepared to be a mother paradoxically turned out to be the very ones that caused my children the most harm. Just think about that for a moment. Could the same be true for you? How would you know? And if there were a way to know the answer, wouldn't you want to?

Before I became a mother, I remember people saying, "You'll see, having children will turn your life upside down," and I thought I was ready for this change. Far from conforming to what many French people still believe, that "you'll have to watch out so that motherhood does not take over your whole existence," I could not wait to see my entire life upended. I was eager to change my habits and way of life so I could devote myself to my children, no matter what I might have to give up. It was this kind of motherhood that I longed for, given how strong I believed my maternal instincts were, and how much meaning I thought having children would give me.

As we all would probably agree, knowing something and experiencing it are two utterly different things. When my children were actually born, neither the conversations I'd had nor the books I'd read prepared me for the incredibly powerful and contradictory emotions that beset me—primarily love and fear, each on a scale I had never experienced before. It started with the instant bond I felt with them: an age-old, primal, animal attachment. This bond was at once joyful and terrifying as it made me realize that I had just embarked on an adventure that would consume me for the rest of my life. Indeed, the intense love I felt for my children was accompanied by an extraordinarily potent, deep, and visceral fear of any harm that might come to them, and this fear radically transformed me because it tinged everything I did and every move I made with anxiety. For a long while, this anxiety prevented me from finding joy in being with my children, so much so that, even when I understood that my fear was toxic, it took considerable time and effort for me to disentangle my emotions and break free of it.

All parents experience the birth of a child in their own ways, but these emotions are almost always so powerful and intimate that people rarely open up about them to their loved ones. Some parents shared with me that they'd had what they initially believed to be unspeakably shameful feelings of panic that they might not connect with their children, or that they might not actually be fit to raise them. I did not experience these particular worries because I was convinced that the intensity of my feelings was a gauge of my maternal love, and that fundamentally, whatever the daily ins and outs of raising my children, this love was all they needed.

I was wrong.

Make no mistake, I did and do love my children. But I was wrong because that powerful feeling that I was so proud of, and which I called and really believed was love, wasn't purely love. Unbeknownst to me, it came with a lot of so-called baggage from my own upbringing. Whatever contradictory or complex feelings I had, I would never harm my children, I assumed, because my protective love for them would always carry the day. It was an innocent enough belief, wasn't it? Isn't this what we all learn about love, in romantic relationships too? That it's magic? A cure-all? Reality teaches us, on the contrary, that love is work—and figuring out what type of work is required of us as parents is no easy task.

As a new mother, I didn't think deep self-awareness was part of the job description. I thought that embodying the behavior of a good mother—acting like a good mom—was what it would take. And all this would require of me, I believed, was making any difficulties or complex emotions of my own invisible to my children.

In other words, to keep my children safe and protected by my love, I was essentially hiding everything else from them in order to present them with the stable and reassuring outward appearance of a responsible adult. I was confident that this approach would give them the stability and sense of safety that they needed, not realizing that far from being convinced and reassured by this superficial and bogus stability, my children could tell that something didn't feel right—and it made them very anxious. Even more troubling than fostering this sense of anxiety in them was that my pretending to be in control of situations and hiding my true emotions was cultivating a sense of falseness in them, and once even made one of them ask me, "Why are you pretending to love us?"

This is what I began to learn—and it was not something I had seen in any books or shared in conversations with other mothers: the very personal way in which we experience parenthood is what determines the nature and quality of the invisible and unspoken connection we have with our children, at least as much, but perhaps even more so than, our practical, day-to-day behavior and interactions with them. I had no idea how much this invisible connection was running the show. And here's what I wish someone had told me back then: that raising healthy, happy children requires us first to recognize, then to discuss and identify, our own emotions—including love, fear, and everything else, and not just the feelings related to our children—so that we can channel these feelings, accept them, drop them, or do whatever we need to do while also finding adequate ways to disclose them to our children. It might be surprising or difficult to believe that a hidden but powerful emotion about, say, an experience from our own adolescence might be affecting the invisible connection with our children, but it just might—in fact, it probably is. Parenting is a practice that, like many practices, requires an ongoing and rigorous study of the self—a developing self-awareness is vital. It might also be surprising or difficult to believe that uncovering and becoming aware of our emotions is hard work. But if it were easy, everybody would already be doing it.

As I learned from parenting in France—and as is certainly the case in the US, and indeed all over the world—our roles as parents raise all sorts of charged discussions. While there may be exceptions, these discussions often rely more on practical topics such as nutrition, educational styles, and so forth than on the intimate way we experience our relationship with our children. I believe this is in part because we lack the necessary markers and guideposts to analyze matters as subtle as our emotional connections. For example, not everyone has a therapist, or the language of a therapist, integrated into their experience. In writing this book, my hope is to begin to include some of these therapeutic markers and guideposts into conversations about parenting.

By now, everyone knows that children need an emotional connection with their parents or primary caregivers.[1] This need for love is real—and necessary—as has been proven by several clinical studies,[2] such as the famous one conducted by Dr. René Spitz that examined 123 abandoned babies, ranging from the age of twelve to eighteen months, who were housed in a facility for children of imprisoned women. This institution was maintained at the highest standards of hygiene, but human contact was avoided as much as germs were. Though the children did receive shelter, food, and clothing, the lack of signs or gestures of affection resulted in symptoms of depression that, in the most severe cases, led to death.[3]

For me as a parent, studies such as this one didn't raise any concern since I felt that, in addition to meeting their physical needs, I had plenty of love to give my children. What I didn't realize was that I had no idea what *kind* of love and attention they truly needed to thrive in all areas of their lives.

As I came to learn, and as many of my friends who are now older parents also came to learn, children are shaped not only by whether or not they receive attention, but also by the kind of attention they receive. Without emotional connection and affective exchange, children cannot become self-aware or learn how to structure their emotions, which are necessary steps for them to develop, and which they'll accomplish by either employing empathy toward the people who surround them, or by reacting against them. If these needs are not met in quantity or quality, children can close themselves off and run the risk of growing up to be shy, awkward, asocial, or mentally ill.[4] We now know, moreover, that the quality of such relationships has a formative effect on children's learning abilities and physical health.[5]

## CHILDREN SENSE EVERYTHING

You're a little worried—though you might never voice it—that your child won't be as attractive as you are. Something terrible happened at work and you're full of feelings of worthlessness. You and your partner don't fight in front of the children and never would, but you're furious with him—just seething with contempt. Your infant might not have the language for any of these things, but he or she "knows" all of it—in a deep and visceral way. Newborn babies are often compared to sponges because they absorb everything—starting with the emotional environment that surrounds them, and particularly their mother's or their primary caregiver's state of mind.[6] No wonder that infants should develop an almost telepathic aptitude. Such a "sixth sense" is necessary for their survival. Adapting to their caregiver is a matter of life or death.

Consider a sixteen-month-old boy who, since birth, slept an excessive eighteen hours a day when under the care of his mother, and a perfectly normal amount of time when cared for by his father. The father eventually discovered the explanation for the child's behavior: the mother was diagnosed with schizophrenia, a condition the child had already picked up on. Having concluded that his mother was incapable of interacting with him or caring for him, the boy knew that for his safety he should learn to do without her attention.

Or consider a friend of mine, Claire, a young mother with a physical disability, whose two-month-old girl wiggled around on the changing table when her father was in charge, but stayed perfectly still when her mother was performing the same tasks, so eager was this infant to make things easier for Claire.

And here's a third example, demonstrating a dynamic similar to the one I was unknowingly fostering in my own children. Morgan, a young mother I knew, thought it was best to keep the death of the family dog hidden from her children, aged five and seven. She was surprised when, days later, she overheard them talking about the dead dog as she was driving them to school. She had to listen closely because, convinced that their mother had not understood that the dog was dead, her children were whispering in the backseat to spare her any pain as they talked about its dead body—wondering aloud if its carcass might be at the neighborhood slaughterhouse that they were passing in front of at that very moment.

The first conclusion to be drawn here is that it is unrealistic to think we can really hide anything from our children. Furthermore, it's a mistake to think we are protecting them by doing so. We are better off expressing our feelings and informing our children of any major problems of ours in plain, age-appropriate language so that they understand they are not responsible either for the problem itself or for coming up with a solution. Sentences such as "Mummy gets sad sometimes" or "Your mother and I are angry with each other right now" can help set children at ease by confirming what they are sensing and by freeing them to turn their attention to other things that interest them.

Without clarifications of this kind, children may feel responsible for the tensions around them. They imagine that we parents depend on them as completely as they depend on us. And since we are responsible for all their difficulties, they feel equally responsible for ours. This is why we so often hear from children some version of "Is it my fault?" This learned feeling of guilt can become so entrenched in them that they have trouble letting go of it as adults. How many of us still feel perpetually responsible for the well-being of our parents, and by extension, for the well-being of any number of people whose problems are neither our fault nor our responsibility?

But there's something more that the example of Morgan really starts to get at: our children not only feel responsible for our problems, they also imagine elaborate scenarios to find explanations for our silences and lies. Consider this seemingly funny and benign example from my own circle of friends: a two-months pregnant young mother decided to wait a little before telling Caroline, her four-year-old daughter, that she would soon have a little brother or sister. This was a wasted effort, as the little girl was already confiding her mother's secret to her babysitter: "My mom has a baby in her tummy, but she doesn't know it." Caroline didn't need her mother to tell her something she already knew, but her mother's silence led her to the only plausible explanation she could find: that her mother didn't yet know she was pregnant.

It doesn't take long to see, however, that such a dynamic is really neither funny nor benign. The confusion our children experience when their feelings do not coincide with our official story can lead them to stifle or adjust their emotions so that they somehow conform to the version we present them with. At other times, they may turn off these emotions altogether to stop their own suffering and confusion. But by silencing their emotions they deprive themselves, often permanently, of an inner compass that is essential to their mental health and judgment. We can't know what difficulties or challenges lie in store for our children, but among the best gifts we can give them to help navigate those challenges is an inner compass that works, and that they can trust and rely on.

In the 1966 film *Misunderstood* (*Incompreso*) by Luigi Comencini, a father believes that the death of his wife will more severely affect his younger son than his older son. He therefore asks the older boy, Andrew, age ten, to say nothing to Miles, his six-year-old brother. Andrew, who is not allowed to express his grief, ends up keeping the pain of this loss inside while outwardly feigning a cheerful and playful demeanor to protect his little brother and respect his father's wishes. As a result, Andrew seems insensitive to his father, who in turn becomes distant toward him and instead gives all his affection to Miles. Meanwhile, Miles, who has understood that his mother will never return, has gotten used to being the sole recipient of his father's attention to the point of falling ill to prevent a little bonding trip that their father had planned to take with Andrew.

In the film's climactic scene, Andrew suffers a deadly fall that opens the father's eyes and heart. With the boy on his deathbed beneath a portrait of his deceased mother, the distraught father finally says, "You are the son that every father would like to have."

## CHILDREN MIMIC EVERYTHING

In addition to absorbing everything like sponges, children imitate everything their parents do. We say we know this and that it's obvious, but the extent to which it is true and real, and what it means in terms of our relationships with them, can still be surprising.

A straightforward example: I know a three-year-old girl, Colette, whose apparent sassiness worried her father. Whenever he asked her to do something, she would shoot back: "What's the magic word?" Initially surprised, he realized that she was repeating word-for-word what those around her told her in instructing her to say "please" when she asked for something. Once he figured this out, he was able to address Colette's sassiness in a constructive way, explaining to her that although she was absolutely right, she should not demand that he or any other adult use the "magic word."

So if our children's behavior presents a problem, shouldn't we begin by examining our own behavior, since their attitudes reflect ours? Some parents—including me, once upon a time—might reply by explaining that one of their children behaves very differently from his or her brothers and sisters, and that this child's misconduct could not be caused by their own child-rearing methods, which were consistent among all their children. Even here our influence may be the root cause; although we might have had the same ideas and intentions in mind, in practice we did not necessarily raise each of our children the same way. We don't remain unchanged as people through each birth of a new child, and each child brings out a singular set of emotions in us. Each child receives a unique set of signals.

## CHILDREN RESPOND TO EVERYTHING

Children read things in us that we don't even know are there. Even if our words state the opposite of our emotions, it's our emotions that guide our children, overriding time and again the words we say to them. These "emotional" messages can be more than simple ones of fear, for example; they can also be elaborate, unconscious messages. Think about that for a moment! Our children are reading and responding to the messages we don't even know we are sending. That's why it's so important to be aware of ourselves—so we can be aware of what our children are picking up on. Practically speaking, as soon as the underlying message you are sending your children and the words you tell them are the same, as soon as there is no conflict between your emotions and your verbal message, your child will follow your instructions and/or wishes right away. At the very least, as parents we must be on the lookout for such unconscious messages, because they provide the key to much of what our children end up doing.

So when our children behave in a disturbing way, we should address the problem at least in part by examining our own fears and unconscious desires. There's a strong chance that a misbehaving child is simply reacting to that invisible influence, since children respond to our mental state. That seems straightforward enough, and who would disagree? But what this actually looks like in day-to-day life might be a little more unexpected. It may be of particular interest to new, young parents to hear a few stories I've collected over the years about how this parent–child dynamic might keep children from sleeping through the night.

Here's a fairly common example. Even at nine months, Zack, the son of a woman I know, was still waking her up three times a night, and she told me that at first she could not see how Zack's crying brought her a sort of relief. After thinking it over, however, this woman admitted that she was terrified by sudden infant death syndrome, and that she needed to hear Zack cry during the night to make sure that he was still alive. In other words, the only wish she was aware of was her "false" wish that Zack would sleep through the night and let her sleep too. In truth, her unconscious desire was for Zack to prove that he was alive. And Zack was obeying his mother's emotional "order" by routinely waking her up.

Or take Amy, whose two-and-a-half-year-old daughter, Lea, had cried every night since her birth. Amy's husband had a heart attack just before the birth of their daughter, naturally leaving Amy frightened at the prospect of her husband dying. Therefore, Lea's cries, which forced Amy to get up several times during the night, would also allow her to check on her husband to make sure he was still alive.

Then there was Natasha, whose five-year-old son, Cedric, also woke up every night. When questioned by her therapist about the possible advantage she might unconsciously be deriving from this behavior, Natasha came to understand that since she worked all day, nighttime provided her with her only opportunity to prove that she was a good mother, without a nanny around. When Cedric would wake from a nightmare, she would comfort him before putting him back to bed, thinking she was attending to her son's needs despite her fatigue. But in fact, she was unconsciously comforting herself, proving to herself that Cedric still needed her, and that she was useful to him. So, by waking her up, Cedric was responding to her unconscious desire by reassuring her that she was a good mother.

A final example is the story of Luke, a baby who screamed every night. His mother, Marina, had recently agreed to conceive a third child to please her husband, Tom. But while Tom was overjoyed about having the new baby, Marina was less so. She perceived this birth as a chaotic change to her own life, which had only gotten back to "normal" once their two older children had become more independent. She resented her husband for not having to share any of the sacrifices she had to make in order to please him, particularly having to stay at home alone all day while he went off to work. So, Luke's endless crying, which also woke Tom at night, gave Marina the opportunity to punish her husband.

For children, especially very young children, everything that comes from their parents—including those signals we're not aware that we're sending—carries the weight of absolute authority. And our children will draw on any and all possible cues to try to make sense of that authority. Explicit statements, casual gestures like a smile, a movement of retreat or tension, or fear—these are things that children notice and process. But they don't grasp linguistic nuances or unstated intentions and they don't perceive the meaning of our words so much as the emotions behind them. The fearful exclamation "You're going to fall!" has the same effect on children as the imperative "Fall!" because they interpret our negative emotions, such as fear, as an order to fail; in contrast, our positive emotions are read as encouragement to succeed.

Perhaps in this sense children are not very different from adults. Imagine describing a project you really care about to a close friend. Now ask yourself how you'd be affected by your friend's reaction. His or her response might even make you doubt, give up, or even fail at this project; alternatively, it might give you a boost or help you develop it further.

Now multiply the impact of these words by a hundred to get an idea of how strongly children are affected by their parents' reactions. Remember: children see us as all-powerful giants. This has the potential to make us incredibly imposing, even frightening. For this reason, we make an imprint wide and deep enough to last well into adulthood, by which time some may need the help of a therapist to reduce it to a more manageable size. That is why, as parents, we have to acknowledge the implicit and explicit authority we have in our children's eyes and understand what it really entails.

Indeed, when we say to our children, "I'm afraid you're failing at school," although we may be well-intentioned, we are unfortunately being harmful; far from warding off the danger, our fear actually sabotages our children's chances to succeed, and pushes them toward failure.

This dynamic is illustrated by the following very French story, which perfectly illustrates our tendency toward a tough love that often simply masks our darker impulses. Ronald was a fifty-year-old banker whose son Leo was an excellent student in his senior year at one of Paris's prestigious high schools. Leo's best friend, Jeffrey, was head of the class. One day, Ronald was speaking with

Jeffrey's father about the brilliant academic future await-
ing their children when the other father, to Ronald's great
surprise, replied skeptically: "Maybe. First Jeffrey needs to
do well at his Baccalauréat" (the equivalent of an SAT).
Ronald found the remark utterly perplexing; how could
Jeffrey's father be so blind to the extraordinary achievement of his son? It turned out that twenty years earlier,
Jeffrey's father had been rejected by Polytechnique (one
of France's Grandes Écoles, prestigious universities analo-
gous to the Ivy League), and that he was still experiencing
the sting of that failure. Doubting his own son's chances
of success unconsciously protected him from feeling like a
failure himself—how could Jeffrey "make it" if he himself
hadn't done so? To put it more bluntly, he had to put down
his son in order to not feel worthless himself. And since
he could not fathom the idea that Jeffrey would succeed
and surpass him, he was subconsciously ordering him to
fail. Ronald learned several months later that this father
had in fact achieved his goal. Almost unbelievably, although Jeffrey managed to do well on the Baccalauréat
and was head of his class, he was not accepted into any
of the Grandes Écoles. While this outcome certainly de-
fied all academic logic, it was wholly consistent with the
psychological logic that drives children of all ages to obey
their parents.

Such seemingly good intentions might fall under the
rubric of "helicopter parenting" that is so common in the
US, but which certainly exists everywhere. We often dis-
parage helicopter parenting, and these examples provide
another reason why we may do so. The constant attention

and care helicopter parents give their children only reveals these parents' fears and their distrust in their children's capacity to meet certain expectations, even when completing simple tasks. This ends up producing high levels of anxiety and low self-esteem in these children.

## WHAT DO WE DO?

It's all very well and good to admit that our emotions as parents influence the development of our children, but what are we to do with this information, given how often it seems impossible for us to control our negative thoughts?

First of all, we should definitely express our emotions—including the ones we consider best kept hidden and unspoken—considering that our children feel them anyway. Another reason to do so is that any attempt we make to conceal our true feelings may put us in such a state of tension that it becomes difficult for us even to take pleasure in our children's company.

Nevertheless, we must abide by some rules. The first rule in my own parenting journey was to try to get some kind of handle on my anxiety. And I succeeded only when I understood that worrying is not a demonstration of love. It appears to stem from love, because it is an inherent part of what we experience as parents, and it can occasionally be a superficial way to show our children how much we care. But in fact, worrying is harmful to them. So I came to understand that I had to show some restraint while manifesting my anxiety, in order not to prejudice my children.

In the same vein, as seems a common practice in the US, we should emphasize the positive by encouraging our children with statements such as "I know you can do it." Why? Because these simple motivations produce incredible results. Daily life shows us that we are regularly seduced by alluring marketing slogans or that we try to inspire others with uplifting blandishments like "Capable as you are, I'm sure you're going to solve my problem" rather than "I suppose there's no point in asking you to solve my problem."

In just the same way, taking a positive approach with our children will boost their emotional resources immeasurably and make them that much more capable of solving problems for and by themselves. The problem with this positive approach, of course, is that one has to believe the enthusiasm one is trying to convey if it's to be taken seriously. Otherwise we're back where we started: giving our children a false message that they instinctively know is untrue, and that they will do mental and emotional acrobatics in an effort to understand.

It is just as important for us to protect our children from negative remarks (which, I am sorry to say, French people use with no shame on the pretext that it builds character), even if others in our circle of friends may consider such comments harmless. For instance, we should avoid making jokes about our children's looks or personality. Even seemingly affectionate nicknames such as "chubby cheeks" can contain all sorts of denigration that damages a child's self-esteem.

It is also important to avoid projecting qualities onto our children. For example, casually saying that a child "resembles Uncle Paul" may have a positive effect if the uncle in question is a Nobel Prize winner but could have a negative impact if he's a compulsive gambler. Also to be avoided are off-the-cuff labels and characterizations such as "She's a real pig," "He's a couch potato," or "All Nicole's kids are smarty-pants," which deprive children of their own space and personality. Such name-calling is often seriously harmful, and in extreme cases can result in the transmission of a physical illness from one generation to the next.

Take Oliver, age five, who caught a cold at his family's summer house. Several other members of the family suffered from asthma, notably a grandfather who, upon hearing his grandson cough, decreed, "Oliver has asthma!" Oliver's father strongly objected to this hasty diagnosis and exclaimed "Certainly not!" Without that sharp reply, Oliver could very well have developed asthma since that condition, like so many, is suspected to be influenced by the power of suggestion.[7]

Unfortunately, children's behavior is also at times interpreted in the light of a preexisting family pathology. Twenty-year-old Christine, for instance, concluded that she should abstain from indulging in puns and other wordplay in order to avoid being suspected of mental disorders. Her mother had been diagnosed as bipolar and those around her noticed she had a tendency to say something humorous just before falling into one of her manic phases. This interpretation was particularly dangerous for Christine since her sense of humor, which might have been admired and praised in any other family, was deemed worrisome in her own. This may have raised her risk of developing the bipolar disorder whose genetic component, it has been shown, expresses itself more under conducive environmental conditions.[8]

In order to stick to a positive approach, we have to rethink our role as educators. We must understand that we are not responsible for fixing every mistake or preventing every failure in our children's lives. We should take enough pleasure in their company to be able to lead them on a patient educational journey, during which we teach them important values while also allowing them to blossom, build their character, and develop their strengths until they are ready to go off on their own.

# 2

❧

# We Repeat Our
# Own Childhood

*Every man has his natural place;*
*its altitude is determined by neither pride nor value:*
*childhood decides.*

—JEAN-PAUL SARTRE,
*Les Mots (The Words)*, 1963

## THE IMPRINT OF CHILDHOOD

If you think you can erase the imprint that your childhood
has left on you simply by force of will, you're as wrong as
I was.

Indeed, the illusion I had about my own abilities as a
parent was not my only illusion. I was also sure I had pro-
cessed my own childhood and distanced myself from it as
best I could. Although I had not undergone therapy, I was
certainly familiar with the basic tenets of psychoanalysis,
whose popularity and influence in France had been fairly
limited in my parents' day, but was the norm for my generation. As a result, I was aware that I had been shaped by
my childhood, but, like many people, I was convinced that
there was no point in dwelling on the mistakes my parents

had inevitably made, or in complaining about the relatively minor troubles I had suffered. I also believed that the best way to erase the residual imprint made by my childhood was to move forward as an adult and live my life. Makes sense, right? After hitting two milestones of adulthood—finding a job and getting married—I felt that having children, which would put me into a different generation, would free me by naturally stripping away any lingering traces of my childhood. I could not have been more wrong.

As I discussed in the previous chapter, a parent's influence on their children is proportional to their power over them. While this influence fades during adolescence as children begin to distance themselves from their parents, it nevertheless leaves an imprint that isn't automatically erased when they grow up. Our childhood continues to manifest and affect us as we get older, shaping our choices in every facet of our lives.

For example, we are often drawn to certain people, places, houses, and smells because, consciously or not, they remind us of our childhood. Indeed, many of these apparent discoveries are recollections, and in truth a number of our supposedly spontaneous reactions stem from our experiences as children. In other words, we are so consumed by our childhood that we re-create its scenarios without even realizing it. One need not be a psychoanalyst to grasp this notion, which is now widely propagated wherever we read about the link between childhood trauma and romantic relationships.[9] Examples are plentiful: the woman who is attracted to older partners because she was affected by her father's absence; the person who falls for Casanovas because they remind him or her of an emotionally unavailable father. Or the man who had an overbearing mother and who is unwittingly attracted to domineering women, or the man whose mother demanded all of his love, and who finds himself unable to commit to the woman in his life.

The French writer Romain Gary remarked, "Had my mother taken a lover, I would not have spent my life dying of thirst near every fountain." The women in Gary's life could not compete with the unconditional love of his mother, who had put him on a pedestal. It is with a mix of gratitude, resentment, and nostalgia that he describes this relationship in *La Promesse de l'Aube* (*Promise at Dawn*, a 1960 book that was made into a film in 1970, and again in 2017).

So this close correlation between our childhood and adult relationships is more or less well known. But the impact of childhood does not end with its consequences on our love life; it makes itself felt in every aspect of our existence, and in countless ways. If we had an extremely stern father, for instance, odds are we will reproduce that situation in adulthood. We may reproduce it in only one dimension of our life, for example by letting ourselves be dominated by our partner at home while being perfectly well balanced at work. Or we may spread this situation to all areas of our lives, finding ourselves victims of a despotic boss and a domineering spouse, as well as of bullying friends who subject us to their strict dietary habits or taste in clothes. But when it comes to parenting, almost all of us will reproduce what we experienced as children, so avoiding this impulse in our approach to parenting is another matter. Why?

In becoming parents, we immerse ourselves once again in the world of childhood *through* our own children, whose experiences inevitably hold up a mirror to our own. This immersion and reactivation of our early life makes its effect on our behavior as parents impossible to avoid. This idea is unbearable. Indeed, admitting the reach of our childhood is easy as long as it affects only us, but it becomes terrifying when we realize that it affects our children as well.

## THE GRIP OF CHILDHOOD: PARENTS UNDER THE INFLUENCE

Like it or not, we have no more control over our role as parents than we do over whom we "choose" to fall in love with. Just as in some measure we fall for partners based on our childhood rather than on our conscious desires as adults, we instinctively model our parenting style on that of our parents, instead of following our own "updated" and conscious ideas on the matter. While this explains why our parenting style is often neither wise nor rational, it does no good for us to blame ourselves. Our difficulties as parents, similar to our poor choices in our love lives, are not the result of bad luck, character flaws, or poor judgment. Rather, these difficulties stem from an ineluctable tendency to replay our own childhood. We are indeed "under the influence" of our childhood and of the ways our parents treated us.

It is this very predisposition that we mistakenly call our "instincts," which in reality are nothing more than a set of unconscious automatic reflexes inherited from our past—our first, knee-jerk reactions regarding how to manage certain situations. In fact, our most questionable involuntary conduct does not correspond to a lack of what we call instinct, but rather to an astonishingly high degree of it; it is what makes us pick the unfaithful spouse out of thousands of possible partners, or adopt our parents' worst behavior and apply it to our own children. It may be painful, but we are better off facing the fact that we can't trust our "instincts."

What I called "trusting my gut" simply meant reproducing my parents' behavior. That's what everybody tells you to do, so that's what I did. I trusted my own first reactions, believing they must be correct, and also because it felt good—it felt like it was what I was supposed to do. So why did I feel just as strongly in agreement with myself when I followed these impulses as I have felt in doubt when I tried to analyze and judge my own parenting skills? The answer is simple. I was drawing the wrong conclusion from a valuable insight: my "instincts" only seemed relevant to me because they led me to reproduce my parents' behavior, which had been embedded in my mind from an early age.

If this sounds familiar to you, then you know how easy it is to equate our familiarity with and reactions to these behaviors with their being "right." The only reason we don't question our behavior or even try to rely on our judgment is because we are convinced we aren't able to, when in reality we lack the necessary benchmarks to imagine and adopt new parenting behavior.

The good news, however, is that it is possible to become the parents we want to be and distance ourselves from our childhood baggage. That's the whole purpose of this book. It is addressed to all of us who are filled with such a hope and ambition, who have already sensed our tendency to reproduce our parents' behavior, and who fear more than anything that we may inflict the same pain upon our children. Yet we have to understand that instead of dismissing this repetition mechanism—as we tend to do because we do not know how to prevent it, or because we believe that merely knowing there is such a mechanism means we are somehow free of it—we instead must constantly keep it in mind in order to fight it, and eventually overcome it.

So how do we detect this so-called mechanism that pushes us to reproduce our parents' behavior? First of all, we need to realize that, far from being exceptional, it's the source of most of our reactions toward our children—so much so that we have to be on the lookout at all times and in all circumstances. This mechanism functions by provoking reactions in us that at first glance appear fair, indispensable, and irrefutable, whereas a closer, rational examination would reveal these same reactions to be superfluous, debatable, or even invalid.

Take my friend Annie, who insisted that her fifteen-year-old daughter drink a glass of milk every day after school, citing the importance of calcium for proper growth. Annie would keep nagging until her daughter gave in, when in reality what she wanted was to discuss much more serious issues, including her suspicion that her teenage daughter was doing drugs. Yet Annie was convinced she was behaving reasonably and doing her parental duty by attending to her daughter's nutrition. Eventually Annie began to evaluate her approach in light of her real values and priorities, and she finally realized that she really didn't care that much about her daughter's consumption of dairy products. What's more, she understood that she was wasting her authority on a trivial matter rather than reserving it for the real issue she should have been dealing with. Annie realized that she was only copying the behavior of her parents who had done the same with her.

This predisposition to do the same as our parents did often shows up as a fixation on some seemingly trivial matter such as obsessing over when children should go to bed, how they should tidy up their room, or what they should be eating. Take the example of parents who put their children to bed at 8 p.m. sharp and who make this bedtime into an ironclad rule. It's likely these parents have never reflected on what they think is a totally reasonable, healthy, character-building rule. It's not even that they fail to question what hidden motive might lie behind it—there is zero awareness that there might *be* any hidden motive behind it. But it would only take a moment's mindfulness to release the hold of their own upbringing on their current parenting: all they would have to do is ask why they are making such a big deal over a relatively minor point in their children's upbringing, why they are so incapable of flexibility (unable, for instance, to adjust the bedtime to particular circumstances or to the number of hours of sleep their children really need), to realize that this has nothing to do with what's best for their children, but instead everything to do with the time at which their own parents sent them to bed when they themselves were children.

It is the same predisposition to repeat unthinkingly that which is familiar (and which we therefore consider "good" or reasonable) that can determine our strengths and weaknesses as parents.

The story of my old friend Yves is a prime example. He had benefited from his well-off father's largesse all his life, so much so that he never had to struggle to make a living. Even though Yves enjoyed the undeniable advantages of his situation, he couldn't help but resent his financial dependency in some measure, and the effects this dependency had upon his growth and evolution as an independent adult. Upon finding himself in a situation identical to his father's when Yves's own son became unemployed, my friend could not keep from helping out financially, knowing full well that he risked depriving his son of the chance to develop the drive necessary to land a job and feel the pride that would come with such an achievement. Yves was compelled to act the way he did even though he knew better.

And it is this same predisposition to repeat our own upbringing that is at the heart of what irritates us or makes us angry with our children's behavior and can even lead us to resort to physical or verbal violence.

This was the case with a therapy patient, Isabelle, who was behind the wheel when her kids started acting up in the backseat, making her so angry that she shouted: "If you don't cut it out, I'm going to smack you!" She realized that this had no effect on her children, who feared neither her nor her threats and continued to play loudly. Watching their total lack of reaction in the rearview mirror, she understood that nothing in the system of values she had instilled in them could in any way make them think that they were doing something wrong, since all they were really doing was being a little rambunctious. So she realized that her threatening behavior was as uncalled for as it was disproportionate. Instead of insisting that they stop, screaming at her kids like she really wanted to, Isabelle pulled over to calm herself down. In that moment it struck her that she reacted the same way every time a similar situation occurred. She made the connection with her father's reaction when she and her brother were acting up as children. Recalling this made her uncomfortable because it brought back the very sharp and specific feeling of confusion and injustice she would feel each time her father got angry for the same reason. She struggled to understand why she would reproduce a behavior that had caused her such pain as a child.

These connections between Yves's and Isabelle's parenting choices and their own childhoods may seem obvious to us, or to anyone from the outside, but we have to remember that—as was the case for me—if such connections were obvious to the parent in question, the behaviors wouldn't be repeated in the first place. The power is in the unawareness and lack of conscious thought that lay behind this dynamic—and every one of us is subject to unawareness and lack of conscious thought. This is what we are up against as parents.

As we become more aware of what is behind some of our parenting behaviors, we need to distinguish this reflexive tendency to repeat our childhood norms from the incredible frustration we all feel at one point or another, the frustration that often surfaces during times of hopelessness or helplessness, as when we are trying to calm a crying baby. In this case, our anger stems from a sudden and irrepressible desire to release ourselves from the crushing weight of our responsibility to our children. The violence of this impulse used to terrify me as much as it made me feel guilty. Fortunately, this frustration was (and still is) widely known as a common reaction among parents. So, for me, the simple fact of being able to acknowledge it decreased its intensity and prevented me from acting on it. In such a situation, a frustrated but responsible parent walks out of the room to calm down instead of shouting or, worse, resorting to violence. But what I'm focusing on here—the tendency to unconsciously repeat our own parents' behavior—has nothing to do with this kind of frustration.

On the contrary, the "repetition mechanism" is difficult to detect because at first, the behavior in which we're engaging doesn't appear bad to us at all. Who wouldn't praise a parent for insisting upon an 8 p.m. bedtime? Or monitoring her child's daily milk intake? In some cases, these repeated, compulsive parenting behaviors can seem wonderful, and sometimes they even are. It's what is behind these rules that is a problem—when you obsess over milk instead of talking about drugs, when you can't change a bedtime rule even if the child is on vacation and wants or needs something that requires a slight adjustment. It's when you're so in thrall to the dynamics of your own childhood that you cannot see your actual child.

Though it may be unintentional, we usually fail to identify our approach as problematic, or even to detect the origins of our behavior, though it is always triggered by very specific scenarios. When it came to my own parenting, I would instead find ways of rationalizing my patterns of thinking and acting. Why would I do such a thing? Why would you?

## THE POWER OF HABIT

The first answer to this question is habit—we never completely get over our own childhood tendency to mimic our parents. Habit can of course be practical and positive, especially when it comes to transmitting what we call our "culture," including all the distinct elements that make up our social environment and that go far beyond the kind of simplistic proclivities that drive us to eat barbecue in the South or clam chowder in Boston. Our tendency to imitate affects our traditions, our heritage, and everything that makes up our identity, even including, sometimes, such subtleties as unexamined ideas about time and the rhythm of our lives.

Take forty-five-year-old Jerome, who one day realized that he had changed jobs or countries every three years since the beginning of his professional life, even though nothing in his career had required him to do so. Up until then he had thought that this was only a coincidence because he had not premeditated any of these changes. At most, he had imagined that he was only reacting to the sense of boredom that would invariably come over him if he stayed for too long in one job or one place. It was only after reflecting on his childhood that he made the connection to his childhood, when he had similarly moved every three years, since a very young age, due to his father's military career. For Jerome, habit manifested itself in a certain feeling of time.

The process of transmitting our culture and values is essential to each of us as parents, because it engages the fundamental instincts that relate to self-reproduction and self-improvement, both of which play vital roles in child rearing. This explains why it is difficult for two parents from different backgrounds to transmit their respective cultures without conflict. How to care for children can become an issue if one parent believes daycare is a good idea (there's a nine out of ten chance that that parent also was in daycare), and the other believes that parents should keep their baby in their own care as long as possible (as his or her parents probably did as well).

## THE UNCONSCIOUS NEED TO UNDERSTAND OUR CHILDHOOD

Transmitting our culture to our children is one thing; unintentionally inflicting the suffering our parents caused us is another and is much more difficult to admit and understand. Our motivations for doing so are multilayered and elaborate, beginning with our need to understand what we experienced as children.

Take a prime example from Orson Welles's *Citizen Kane*. In a series of flashbacks, this classic film retraces the life of a billionaire megalomaniac who dies alone in his unfinished palace, whispering "Rosebud" with his last breath. The journalist who investigates the meaning of this word goes over many moments in the life of Charles Foster Kane. After a happy childhood, Kane is abruptly taken from his mother and handed over to the care of a banker. Kane is forced to immediately transition from child's play to adult business, and then to empire building, coming close to becoming president of the United States. In rapid succession, he loses his first wife, whom he divorces, his son, who dies in a plane accident, and his mistress-turned-second-wife, who also asks for a divorce—each loss reviving the early abandonment that ruined Kane's life. Among Kane's personal possessions the journalist discovers a toy sled on which is written the word "Rosebud"—the same sled that Kane was playing with when he was taken away from his mother. Though by many measures his life looks successful, it never really distances him from this toy, a symbolic memory of his past life and painful childhood.

Although we may feel as though we have turned a page on our past, certain events from our childhood continue to torment us quietly, even if they were not objectively traumatic. After all, the seriousness of a particular event is sometimes less painful for children than the confusion they feel when they don't understand what is happening and are assailed by feelings that they can neither define nor control. In such cases, children have no choice but to repress their emotions. But in one way or another, repressed emotions resurface long after they have seemingly disappeared.

These feelings often arise when we experience situations as a parent that parallel ones from our childhood. Once reactivated, the confusion we felt as a child begins to torment us like an unsolved crime: What really happened during our childhood? Just as an investigator would reconstruct a crime scene in order to solve the case, we feel the need to reproduce the circumstances of our childhood to reevaluate them, but this time using the judgment and emotional maturity of an adult.

This may seem obvious, but it's common to encounter adults who were beaten as children and who may feel the need to abuse their own children in turn—in large part to confirm that they were in fact beaten. By making acts of abuse real and present in their lives in this way, these parents are unconsciously proving to themselves that their own experience of abuse wasn't just a dream (for they cannot help but doubt the abuse they were a victim of, no matter how real or blatant). Abuse seems even more difficult to understand if what these individuals felt as children was contradicted by what their parents told them. This is often the case with violent parents who loudly declare their love for their children, insist that they are beating them for their own good, or because of some wrongdoing, or, conversely, pretend as though the abuse never happened in the first place. These parents' messages are confusing to the children, provoking an uneasiness that may torment them their whole lives, whereas if these same violent parents had beaten their children in the same way, but admitted that they were at fault, or better yet, apologized, they would have given their children a chance to overcome the trauma.

Believing their parents to be infallible, children conclude that they themselves must be wrong when their impressions don't match what they are told. But how could it be otherwise? As discussed in Chapter One, children depend so much on their parents that they have no choice but to trust them. When children are abused, they scramble their perception of the situation and alter their judgment so as to prove their parents right. Small wonder then that as adults we feel the need to reexamine our past to gain clarity.

This was my neighbor Manuel's story. He realized that he constantly berated his son, but never had any problems with his eldest daughter. It became clear to him that the birth of his son, unlike that of his daughter, had reopened old wounds. When he was five years old, following the revelation of an affair his father was having, Manuel's mother had committed suicide; the day after her funeral, his father asked him to call his mistress "mommy." Manuel refused, and his father accused him of being mean, beginning a pattern of relentless criticism that continued for years.

Although Manuel felt mistreated, he was much too vulnerable to challenge his father's words, and it was too frightening to imagine his father actually being wrong. Without going so far as to adapt to the negative image his father had projected onto him (as unfortunately a large number of children often do in such cases), from then on, Manuel was convinced that he was hard and cruel. The psychologist who counseled Manuel was primarily concerned with getting him to objectively see the wound his father had inflicted. Only once Manuel saw this was he able to understand that he was not a "mean" person, and never had been. He was thereby able to decouple his behavior from the "mean" label and treat his own son more gently.

In so many of these stories, it can seem obvious to outsiders when old wounds are being reopened and harmful behavior repeated. But when it comes to the matter of our own specific lives and stories, there is nothing more difficult for an adult than questioning one's parents—especially when none of one's feelings as children point to one's parents as the source of emotional difficulty. This is why it took Manuel some time before he recognized his father's mistake, and also explains his childhood inability to judge his father's behavior, which seemed to him incomprehensible once he became an adult. Manuel's therapist came up with an analogy to help him understand:

Everyone knows the Eiffel Tower is in Paris, so if a friend tells you it's in Milwaukee, you'll simply think he's talking nonsense. But you only react this way because you're an adult. You are free to believe or dismiss what your friend has said; you could also ask a third party to confirm or refute it. But things would be entirely different if you were a child and it was your mother who was telling you that the Eiffel Tower is in Milwaukee. In that case, even though you know it's in Paris, and you really think you're right, it's more than likely that you'll choose to believe your mother so as not to doubt her word. Later in life, you might need to hear it clearly stated that the Eiffel Tower is indeed in Paris in order to formally contradict your mother and validate what you felt was true when you were a child.

## THE UNCONSCIOUS NEED TO PROVE OUR PARENTS RIGHT

Our other chief motive for trying to prove our parents right is love—both the love we have for them and the love we expect and need from them. This love we felt as children rarely goes away simply because we grow up. As adults, we continue to love our parents and to want to be loved by them; we even continue to fear them. We may go so far as to congratulate ourselves for not bringing up their mistakes—I certainly did. I convinced myself that passing judgment on my parents would serve no purpose.

But these assumptions can have disastrous consequences for us, and not only as parents. In order to avoid judging our parents and, as a result, avoid conflict with them, we often overlook their shortcomings, much as a passenger would in a taxi driven by a lousy driver. Some passengers in this situation would rather try to convince themselves that the driver is fine than face the terrifying notion that they might actually be in danger. As a result, we may justify our parents' behavior with statements like: "My father was right to beat me," or "He meant well," or "It wasn't all that bad."

For me, reassurances of this kind made it even easier to keep hiding the influence of my childhood from myself. Of course, such denial only aggravated my own suffering, which then, having never been taken into account, turned into an increased need to replay it with my own children. The best way to affirm that my parents were right after all was to reproduce their behavior. An endless cycle!

Consider the disturbing fate of Whitney Houston's daughter, Bobbi Kristina Brown, who was found unconscious from an overdose in her bathtub, and later died— thus replicating the exact same circumstances of her mother's death three years earlier.

Cases of children reproducing their parents' behavior are as old as humanity itself. We may recall the Greek myth of Kronos, son of Gaia and Uranus, who at the request of his mother castrates his tyrannical father and takes his place on the throne. An oracle had then predicted that one of Kronos's children would do the same and dethrone him, thus prompting him to devour his children, all except Zeus, who had been hidden away by his mother, Rhea, and later defeated Kronos, fulfilling the prophecy.

Refusing to pass judgment on our parents may very well cause us to repeat exactly what they did. We may beat or emotionally abuse our children just as our parents did or choose a partner who will do it for us. It locks us into a vicious cycle of repeating the past, which can span generations. Most of us, probably and fortunately, were not beaten as children, but all childhood suffering has an impact.

Consider my friend Fanny who, as a girl, had decent, respectable parents, each of whom worked fifty to sixty hours a week to provide for the family. As a result, Fanny and her sisters had to let themselves into an empty home at the end of each school day, prepare their own meals, do their homework, and keep themselves occupied until evening. This may have fostered many good characteristics for these children, and who would judge the parents for working hard to provide for the family? But what amounted to some measure of neglect made Fanny and her siblings believe they were unlovable—defective somehow. And each of them chose partners who were either workaholics, emotionally cold, dismissive, or a combination of all three.

## THE VICIOUS CYCLE

We may not be aware of having suffered during our childhood, especially if we didn't allow ourselves to feel pain at the time. As adults, we should therefore pay special attention to our recurring and unwelcome conduct, since it likely stems from this early suffering and could reveal past circumstances that troubled us.

This was the case for Geraldine, who was only attracted to unavailable or indifferent men. Although Geraldine considered her childhood perfectly normal, this repeated behavior signaled a problem. When Geraldine was little, her mother took very good care of her, and her father worked and traveled. When he was home, he was often tired, or continued to work, and he devoted the energy he had left to his wife. Geraldine had no siblings, and her father left the childrearing to his wife. Nothing about this situation felt odd or out of place; Geraldine didn't know what her female friends' relationships were like with their own fathers, and assumed most men left the raising of daughters to their wives. Yet well into adulthood, she found herself recreating the same scenario: she'd choose an indifferent romantic partner, or one who gave his best to another woman (whether a mother or a rival)—all in the misguided hope of finding a man who would finally notice and value her.

In many situations, related to parenting and otherwise, it is important to uncover past suffering, which inevitably continues to manifest itself as long as it has not been recognized and confronted. Otherwise, we find ourselves repeating painful scenarios, trapped in a vicious cycle that offers no way for us to come to terms with our past, let alone heal. Indeed, the only outcome of re-creating these early situations and behaviors with people who resemble our parents is to repeat the same drama that caused us pain in the first place.

Geraldine finally came to see that she had long felt but not understood the pain of having had an indifferent father, and that unless she changed, she would have no chance of finding an attentive and loving partner who could help to heal her childhood wounds. Her therapist suggested that she imagine her father was not indifferent, but blind, and that rather than ask him for attention, Geraldine ask her father—a blind man—to tell her the color of her T-shirt. When her blind father would inevitably be unable to answer her question, Geraldine was to visualize herself seeking out all the blind men she could find to ask the same question. Such an impossible and heartbreaking quest! Geraldine understood that she had to rethink her approach: Should she conclude that her T-shirt was colorless, or that she was better off asking someone who could see?

# THE UNCONSCIOUS NEED FOR REVENGE

Suffering is not the only childhood emotion we suppress and unconsciously reproduce. Resentment also inevitably accompanies our wounds and often arises when we least expect it, such as when we try to give our children that which we did not receive ourselves.

This was the case with Roger, who was abandoned by his parents at the age of three and who sought therapy when his wife became pregnant with their little boy. He realized he wouldn't be able to take care of his son the way he should, because he couldn't help being jealous and thinking that there was no reason his little boy should have a father when he himself had been deprived of one.

Roger's behavior may be difficult to accept, but it is far from unusual. What we lacked or missed out on feels so unfair to us that we derive a false sense of justice from subjecting our children to a similar experience, or by predicting that they too will struggle in the same way.

For example, I once saw a mother and daughter in a dressing room in a department store. The daughter was trying on skinny pants, and the mother, who was overweight, told her: "You'd better wear them now because in a few years you'll be too fat." With this comment, the mother condemned her daughter to follow in her footsteps and gain weight because the mother didn't want to be alone in her ordeal.

By unconsciously avenging the "injustices" of our childhood, we seek above all to relieve our suffering. But since we are still incapable of attacking the real culprits (our parents)—even symbolically by secretly blaming them— we transfer our anger onto our children and justify our behavior with statements such as, "There is no reason that he or she should have more or anything better than I."

One book that illustrates this is *Vipère au poing* (*Viper in the Fist*, 1948), a novel by Hervé Bazin. Jean, eight years old, and his older brother, Ferdinand, lead a blissful childhood in their paternal grandmother's rundown castle. When their grandmother dies, they impatiently await the return of their parents and younger brother, Marcel, who were living in China. But when she arrives home, their mother turns out to be cold, disdainful, and cruel. She immediately imposes a quasi-military kind of life and brings out such hatred in them that eventually they attempt to poison and drown her.

This hatred lasts until Jean, realizing he is becoming as malicious as his mother, whom he has nicknamed "Folcoche" (from *folle*, meaning "crazy," and *cochonne*, meaning "pig"), runs away to his maternal grandmother, who reveals that she never loved her daughter. During this ordeal, and despite the hatred he feels for his mother, Jean identifies with her and knows he will ultimately end up just like her.

In other words, we exact revenge on our children. The word may seem strong; however, far from being restricted to pathological cases or to the heroes of Shakespearean tragedies, vengeance is a behavior that affects everyone, from the employee who doesn't dare challenge his boss but lets off steam by taking it out on an intern, to the siblings who fight with one another instead of confronting their parents.

The terrible fact is that directing this anger toward our children gives us absolutely no relief. In the same way that a letter needs to be sent to the correct address for it to reach the right person, it is essential to direct the message to the person who is truly responsible for the suffering—our parents—if we are to find any sense of peace. This doesn't necessarily mean that we need to confront them openly; it is enough to do so symbolically by acknowledging what we see as their wrongdoings.

If we were beaten, for example, the real transgression is not to start fighting with our parents, but rather to behave differently and become better parents than they were. This is a fundamental, symbolic protest against their past behavior. By contrast, taking revenge on our children by beating them as well will be interpreted by our parents as a form of homage; after all, imitation is the highest form of flattery. This can explain why our parents so often urge us to do as they did in all areas of life, especially how we raise our children.

The act of disobeying our parents is therefore radical and constructive. It constitutes the only salutary sort of revenge we can hope to get: being freed from our childhood and overcoming our anger rather than taking it out on our children.

**PART TWO**

# ENDING
# THE VICIOUS
# CYCLE

# 3

⨯

# Neutralizing Our Pain

*A proverb reads: "Like father, like son."*
*Another: "Miserly father, prodigal son."*
*Which to believe?*

—ALPHONSE ALLAIS

One of the reasons for my relative confidence in my abilities as a mother in the early days of parenthood lay precisely in my awareness of what is said and is implied in Alphonse Allais's proverb. I knew that I had to watch out for the fact that I was probably like my mother, even though my notion of this similarity was only vague, because I had never studied genetics or psychology. It seemed obvious to me that I would naturally be tempted to repeat the upbringing she had given me. I therefore thought that, in order to become what I deemed a good mother, I simply had to do the antithesis of the things I had not liked about her parenting style, and thereby become her opposite, like the prodigal son of the miserly father.

I soon realized it was not that simple—and for a couple of major reasons. First, it is unbelievably difficult to do the opposite of what we have experienced, and to implement good ideas that bear no relation to the reflexes we have learned from our own past. Furthermore, I soon discovered that I did not have the free will that I thought I did when I was reading the judicious advice offered by parenting books. In fact, many times I did not react to my children at all as I—having carefully absorbed this judicious advice—had decided I would. I might, for example, decide to take a hard line with my children, then find myself comforting them despite my best intentions. Similarly, when I had resolved to be calm and indulgent, I often ended up raising my voice at them and being irritable. I found all of this deeply distressing.

Let me explain this carefully, lest you automatically assume you are or would be better at taking good parenting advice than I was. Imagine that you are driving a car, and you want to turn right because you believe it is the correct direction. So with natural purpose you turn the steering wheel to the right and inexplicably—imagine the terror of such a thing!—the vehicle goes left. It's like a waking nightmare! You realize then that your car does not obey you—it has its own agenda. Sometimes it goes left, sometimes it goes right. It doesn't do what you intend to do or what you tell it to do. And even if it may go the way you wanted to (after all, none of us is wrong 100 percent of the time!), you only have chance, not your own intentions or skills, to thank.

So to return to my early parenting experience, it's not that I was incapable of understanding when to be strict with my children and when not to be. The wonderful thing about doing the opposite of your parents is that it seems so easy and straightforward. You don't have to read or reflect very deeply at all. What happens when you try to actually implement this "opposite" strategy, however, is that it doesn't work. Instead you end up doing something that your unconscious has decided to do. Consider a situation in which, say, a young daughter is telling you about quarreling with her friends at school. It's a situation that calls for comforting and soothing, but she is describing it to you in a shrill and tearful manner, whining at such a pitch it hits your nerves just so, and frays them a little. This visceral and unconscious irritation is the place from whence you end up responding, and that irritation colors your response, perhaps even leading you to raise your voice at your daughter. You did not make a conscious choice to react like this, and you know it is not at all the correct reaction to her distress.

This is of course a relatively mild, everyday example— it's not a huge issue, and your daughter will not be traumatized by it, but you've missed an opportunity to share, relate, advise, or reassure her. In other words, you missed an opportunity to parent in a wise, warm, and constructive way, so you let her down. Furthermore, a "tiny bad thing" such as this becomes a real problem if it's happening every day, or with any kind of regularity.

For a long time as a young mother, I felt stranded—I would even say trapped—between the reflexes I had inherited from my childhood and my intention to do the opposite of things that had caused me suffering. Nor could I find a solution, because I had not yet grasped that by wanting to do the opposite of what my parents had done, I was on precisely the wrong track. In fact, this very decision to "do the opposite" indicated that I still had a long way to go in reconciling myself to my own experiences as a child. Indeed, contrary to my own assumptions, I was so weighed down by these unresolved grievances that I was only focusing on myself and my wounds in this determination to treat my own children differently. What my children needed and deserved was an upbringing designed to suit their own needs and best interests, irrespective of my particular feelings about my childhood. I didn't realize this until much later, whereupon I completely changed my behavior toward them.

The relationship between parents and children is so powerful that often it shapes us permanently and defines who we become as adults, either giving us strength and balance or instilling weaknesses in us and causing us pain. No wonder that reproducing our childhood patterns may be constructive and even convenient if we were fortunate enough to have had good parents, but proves disastrous and feels awful if we were not.

The only way to break these cycles of harm, rooted in our own upbringing, is to heal the wounds we sustained when we were children.

Indeed, this pain is so powerful and long-lasting that the prospect of reconnecting with our childhood or inflicting our own past experiences onto our children terrifies some people to such an extent that they opt out of becoming parents altogether, rather than risk reactivating old wounds, or inflicting them upon potential children of their own. It takes far less than experiencing egregious abuses for a person to feel negatively affected enough by their emotional past to justify not having their own children. Lack of attention and love alone can be enough to prevent a person from fully developing through adolescence, and can later create the need to compensate in adulthood. Or, to provide another example, being put in a position of raising younger siblings at too early an age for such a responsibility may eliminate any desire some of these former children have to repeat the experience as adults.

But choosing not to have children is in fact *not* the most common reaction; most adults who were in various ways and to various degrees mistreated as children are nevertheless likely to have children of their own. And their way of dealing with the past, which they don't know how to break away from, is to push it far into the back of their minds and avoid thinking about it at all costs.

## DOING THE OPPOSITE OF OUR PARENTS

Among those who do have children, there are people who, like me, refuse to repeat the behavioral patterns and dynamics we were subjected to while growing up and decide to face the fact that we may nevertheless be prone to doing so. To make sure we won't harm our children similarly, we decide to break the cycle of harm by doing the opposite of our parents. That's what I did, anyway. My decision, deeply rooted in my own pain, was a very solemn one, and became a sort of personal mantra. Even though I kept it to myself, it was my one and only principle in terms of parenting, and I relied on it alone to guide me in my daily role as a parent. I know now, as I imagine you do, that many,

many people make similar solemn vows to do the opposite of their parents.

If we had flawed parents we are afraid we might mirror, it isn't surprising that this approach reassures and sways us. Without going so far as to believe it will make us good parents, we are convinced it will at least make us better parents than our own. And there may be some truth to that.

Undeniably, those of us who opt for this approach want to do well by our children. It is to our credit that we do everything in our power to avoid abusing our children if we ourselves were abused, or to be attentive if we were ignored, or to remain sober if we grew up in an alcoholic household. In most cases we feel we can rely on this fairly simple approach insofar as it doesn't require us to question the way we parent.

Nevertheless, it's a lot tougher than we think to successfully do the opposite of what was done to us. Often, it means trying to outsmart the unconscious. Simply deciding that we will give our children an upbringing antithetical to our own isn't enough to offset deep-rooted assumptions and behavior. As a result, a lot of parents don't manage to pull it off, despite their best intentions.

As I've stated, this was the case for me, at least at first. And it was also exactly the case for my friend Mary, for whom the decision had much sadder consequences. Since Mary's mother thought only of herself, Mary wanted instead—lofty a goal as it was—to think only of her children. She tried to be as attentive, flexible, and calm as possible with them, since her mother had been distant, unyielding, and angry. But this approach quickly turned out to be much more complicated than Mary had expected because she didn't instinctively know what was good for her children. Having never had a good mother, she lacked the necessary benchmarks. When Mary realized that she was capable of having the same tantrums as her mother, she became convinced that she was toxic to her children. She withdrew from their lives, blindly entrusting them to their father, who had had a happy childhood, firm in her belief that they would be better off without her being too involved. She ultimately understood that this withdrawal was equivalent to her mother's neglect, a continuing source of suffering, and would only inflict the same wounds on her children.

It was a similar story for Zelda, age thirty-two, a French patient who felt that throughout her whole childhood she'd been used as a foil by her mother, a narcissistic, ambitious, and unpredictable actress who appeared fun and eccentric in public but was violent and tyrannical in private. This situation was so painful for Zelda that she determined to become the exact opposite of her mother both intellectually and emotionally. She applied herself to being a sweet and devoted mother and, at least initially, when her daughter was a baby, felt she was for the most part successful. However, once her daughter hit the "terrible twos," Zelda came to the frightening realization that, in moments of heightened stress, she felt instinctively inclined to use physical force. Devastated that she was so conditioned by her childhood and seemingly "fated" to be violent, she joined a cult.

This decision was both baffling and painful to those around her, but to her it made perfect sense: the guru's influence, which relied on strict and highly codified rules about how to raise children, allowed her to free herself from reproducing her mother's poor parenting, which she wanted to avoid at any cost.


As the cases of Mary and Zelda tragically reveal, though we may have the best of intentions and totally understandable motives in trying to give our children what we did not receive, doing the exact opposite of our parents can prove to be absurd and even harmful. It's easy to imagine the detrimental results such a philosophy can lead to if we push this reasoning to the brink: imagine a parent deprived of vitamin C during his childhood, who forces his children to down gallons of orange juice every day. Or another who refuses to discipline his children in any way, even letting them cross the street without holding hands, just because he himself was constantly restrained during childhood. Or, without going quite so far, imagine the more common and realistic situation of a mother who wanted but was never able to take music lessons as a child, and now insists that her son play the piano.

You might ask, "What's wrong with that?" And for good reason. After all, from an educational standpoint, insisting that children play the piano makes good sense; we may think it important for them to play a musical instrument, or that they practice some daily discipline, or perhaps it's part of a family tradition. What makes the behavior of this music-deprived mother questionable is that it shows how much her own childhood continues to have a painful hold

on her. To the extent that this is true, her parenting decisions are all about her, her own upbringing and her own
regrets, rather than about her son and his interests, which
don't even cross her mind. So we thereby see how easy it
is as parents to fall into this trap of repeating exactly what
we intend not to: by doing the opposite of her parents, by
forcing her son to play the piano instead of simply offering him the option, the mother in this example ends up in
fact doing the same exact thing as her parents: disregarding
what her child really needs or wants.

In short, this "contrarian" approach is often the sign of
parents who remain burdened by their own childhood—
and it isn't likely to do them or their children any good
whatsoever.

A friend of mine, Victoria, once burst into tears following an incident at the playground between Benjamin, her
two-year-old son, and the father of a little girl who caused a
scene over a shared toy. Why was Victoria so upset? She had
the sense that she had failed to stand up for her little boy
while he was being harshly reprimanded by a stranger. As
soon as this unknown father began to raise his voice, Victoria swept her son away from the sandbox to protect him
from the man's unwarranted verbal attack. In doing so, she
spared Benjamin from being further exposed to the man's
bad temper; this was a perfectly appropriate reaction on her
part. So why did she feel so distressed and even guilty?

Victoria only understood her feelings once she realized
that, in fact, she was crying over her own childhood, when
no one had defended her. And it was her very own deprivation that she was processing through her son, using him in

an unconscious effort to heal her own childhood wounds. And some part of her knew it. Although this particular episode had not harmed her son, Victoria realized that exploiting Benjamin in this way and making parenting more about herself than about him could do him real harm—and she was right.

What are we to make of all this? Although our decision to adopt this contrarian "do the opposite of my parents" approach may be rooted in a genuine and generous desire to prevent our children's suffering, we are paradoxically similar to those who reproduce the mistakes of their own parents without questioning themselves. We are likewise unable to overcome our childhood, which, like two sides of the same coin, works for some of us as a deterrent, and for others as a guideline.

Important to note here are those parents who adopt contrarian approaches for much more overtly selfish reasons. In some cases, people decide to do the opposite of their own parents with no thoughtful parenting philosophy or good intentions at all—instead, the decision is entirely about healing themselves. In this case, reacting to their own childhood ends up giving them an excuse for shamelessly using their children as props in their emotional dramas. And this is all the more monstrous because it is useless and doomed to fail.

Catherine, for example, was unloved by her mother as a child, and consequently surmised that this wound could be healed by her own daughter Anabelle's unconditional love. And since this desire was rooted in love, it seemed harmless and even moving to those around her, rather than appalling as it should have appeared. All the more so since Catherine's thirst for love could never be quenched by anyone save the person who had deprived her of it in the first place: her mother. Asking Anabelle to fill this void was asking her to do the impossible, effectively setting the little girl up to fail at something she would rightly perceive as being very important to her mother. To say nothing of the unconscious damage Catherine was causing her by asking for constant, exclusive, and never-ending love. Like a devoted nurse, Anabelle, fearing her mother's fragile state, did exactly as Catherine asked and ultimately gave up on any chance of having a life of her own.

My neighbor Jack's parents were similar. They deliberately chose to spend their retirement "enjoying" (following) their thirty-year-old son to compensate for the abandonment they had each experienced from their own parents. It's horrifying to reflect on the impulse behind their behavior: the desire to "enjoy" their son the way a person might enjoy a dessert. Jack couldn't go on vacation without his parents offering to accompany him. He couldn't even go to a restaurant or a concert with friends without his parents wanting to come along and befriend everyone. In the end, he couldn't create a life for himself without this seemingly friendly and convivial parental hovering, which in truth was a disrespectful intrusion into his existence, and a dynamic closer to harassment than to love.

However, there is a world of difference between these toxic extremes of Anabelle and Jack's parents doing the opposite of what they experienced to suit themselves, and the rest of us who believe that the best way to raise our children is to do so because we cannot let go of our childhood and its pain.

Ultimately, our central mistake is to base our children's upbringing on our own wounds rather than on our children's interests, needs, and desires—just as I initially did. But in order to be able to take the focus away from ourselves, we first have to address our own, intrinsically selfish need to heal, which inevitably interferes with our children's best interests. And the only way to do that successfully is to neutralize the negative effects of our childhood.

## MAKING SENSE OF OUR CHILDHOOD

As I learned, my childhood stayed with me for years and years, even without my realizing it. And it influenced my parenting style so much that it often took the reins in spite of my conscious inclinations. Though I truly believed otherwise, it was wishful thinking for me simply to tell myself that I had put my childhood behind me. What I came to understand—and I wish I had known sooner—is that the only way to break free of the cycle of repeating the past is to make sense of and come fully to grips with one's childhood, filtering it and getting rid of its toxic elements in order to transmit only the positive aspects to our children.

How? The answer is both as radical and simple as it sounds: by talking about it. More specifically, by conjuring up our childhood in conversation with a trusted relative, spouse, or therapist. For me, and for many of the friends and fellow parents with whom I have spoken about this, undertaking this process helped me process my emotions and even discover them, by pulling things out of the dark with a rope of language. It helped me clarify my ideas, and retrieve forgotten or buried memories that I would have never formulated on my own, or that I would have continued to leave unsaid, like ellipses within my thoughts. Such work is crucial because it is precisely in these gaps that our unconscious mechanisms are lodged.

## Revisiting Our Childhood

The purpose of this introspective conversation with someone you trust is to take an inventory of your childhood, to determine the good and the bad, and thus to pass judgment on your parents. I know how that sounds and how it makes many of us cringe: passing judgment on our parents. Many of us initially refuse to do so, whether out of love, loyalty, fear of opposing our parents, or some other reason. Quite often, we have the feeling that our parents did their best, that we don't want to "throw stones," that we're not sure we could have done any better in their place, or that we think that finding fault with them serves no purpose. None of these arguments, however, should stop us from establishing a list of what we see as our parents' successes and failures. The objective of this exercise need not involve confronting our parents with what they did wrong, even if they were monsters to us. The goal is to take the necessary steps back that will allow us to overcome our childhood traumas and heal our wounds.

We may even start by listing what was positive about our childhood. For example, the list might include very specific things such as the way our father shared his knowledge of botany with us by taking us mushroom hunting, or how he made us fall in love with literature, carpentry, or tennis. Or it could be more general, such as our mother's steadfast defense of her children when we were unfairly attacked or threatened, whether by peers or teachers, or if she had a healthy attitude toward food. Or perhaps our parents' approach to sexuality was well balanced, devoid of prudishness yet respectful of our privacy and theirs.

Once we have established our impartiality and loyalty to our parents, we can allow ourselves to criticize the negative aspects of the upbringing they gave us.

But this is the toughest part, even on a therapist's couch. It seems to me this might be tougher still in the US, where individuality and autonomy are paramount, and we're taught to move on, move forward, and that each adult should see him- or herself as the sole agent of their own happiness and success, irrespective of family and community.

Whether in Europe or the US, most patients in therapy easily discuss their parents' minor flaws. But they almost always find it inappropriate, whiny, disrespectful, indecent, or grotesque to relate the various emotional cuts and scrapes they feel they received. Why? Because they think it's only legitimate to accord importance to the most severe types of mistreatment—cases of children locked away in closets for years, or repeatedly raped, starved, or beaten.

In the absence of experiences that extreme, some find it very difficult to "throw around" the term "abuse." Most justify seemingly minor torments with thoughts such as, "Nothing unusual about the way my parents behaved";

"Don't all kids have to deal with such things?" or "That's just the way things were back then."

## Acknowledging Abuse

Although the main characteristic of abuse is that it causes lasting pain, most of us who were abused are not aware of it. If anything, we feel guilty ("I brought it on myself") for the mistreatment we received, and we do not connect the abuse we experienced to the problems and difficulties it triggered. Indeed! We attribute our problems and difficulties to our own personality or character instead. And the idea that the more difficult aspects of our personalities or characters might be linked to abuse never even occurs to us.

So let's start with this very fundamental and critical question: What is abuse? It can be a one-time episode but is often the repeated behavior of a parent attempting to dominate or control a child. So abuse shouldn't be defined only by the violence of the gesture or act, but also by what is *driving* the parent. If, for instance, some parents find a symbolic way of spanking—administering a gentle tap on their child's hand or even on his or her bottom—this punishment needs to be understood as part of a larger code. You may think, as I do, that even such "symbolic" spanking is a bad idea, but it's not abuse because it doesn't belie a malevolent impulse and it doesn't usually cause lasting pain. It is the same thing in the case of people who have been spanked or beaten once or twice in their childhood because they have been caught stealing or lying. Chances are that in adulthood these people will not particularly remember the pain of being spanked because their parents

probably resorted to physical violence out of feeling help-
less or powerless, not out of any wish to hurt them.

On the other hand, if a child has been spanked or
beaten or abused verbally or emotionally *repeatedly*, or as
a usual parental response to the child's behavior, chances
are this parent's behavior is indeed abusive, because it involves some kind of humiliation or cruelty that the parent
takes satisfaction in, either shamelessly or under the cover
of discipline. And it prevents the child from blooming, developing appropriately, and thriving.

Abuse can be subtle and it of course does not always or
only manifest physically. Abuse can also be verbal, emotional, mental. Whatever form it takes, it's a behavior that
produces trauma and—I'll say it again—causes lasting
pain. Having lasting pain is one sure sign that allows us to
realize that we have been abused. But it is not the only one.
Indeed much of the time, what we call our "personality"
(or at least, the negative aspects of it) reflects some kind
of abuse in our past. This may seem far-fetched, but that is
only because it's not obvious.

Imagine a boy whose mother blames him for a terrible back injury incurred during pregnancy and delivery.
The child always feels the guilt of having been the source
of his mother's physical handicap. Chances are this psychological load would generate what is called "the guilt of
innocents," meaning the child lives in a constant state of
guilt, burdened with feeling responsible for everything. So
much so that at school, for example, if he sits in the back of
the classroom where another child dropped his pencil box
and is scolded by the teacher, he will feel that it's certainly

his fault, that he must have distracted his classmate with a random gesture or word without realizing it. He may even create elaborate storylines to explain *how* it was his fault. In short, the boy sees himself as guilty in order to justify why his mother disliked or abandoned him. In fact, even decades later, in his fifties, when his mother is no longer around to punish him for it, this now grown man has developed a pattern of sabotaging his own work and relationships. He may just think he is a personal failure, but the current behavior is linked to the old childhood guilt of having been the source of a problem or pain. And if you're guilty, you deserve punishment—you have grown and developed as a human being believing it. This adult will find *and create* reasons (losing job after job, destroying relationship after relationship) to explain his inherent "badness." As with this example, if someone is sabotaging themselves in their career, you can be sure it comes from somewhere, from something shelved in the past.

Abuse can be made even more tricky to detect by the fact that as children, we may have done our best to suppress or deny our pain—and may in fact have been so successful in doing so that we no longer feel the sensation that usually accompanies suffering and signals the fact that we have actually been abused.

Imagine a child victim of repeated verbal abuse who trains himself not to feel the pain in order to withhold from his parents the satisfaction of upsetting him. Or perhaps he trains himself not to feel the pain simply to be able to endure the treatment without feeling constantly upset. As a result, that child "toughens up" successfully, much like someone who has trained himself to leave his hand on a hot stove without feeling the pain. Chances are when this child grows up, he will try to distance himself from his childhood and minimize his parents' faults, leading him to believe that he probably deserved such treatment, which was nothing but ordinary reprimand, and he thereby dismisses the idea of abuse. All of this explains why so many of us may not be able or willing to admit of abuse in our past.

But how can we detect among our feelings the pain that usually validates the abuse if we are not able to feel it? In any similar case of denying abuse, we must understand that this pain is nevertheless manifesting itself through different dysfunctional behaviors of ours, such as acting out for no apparent reason, being stingy, a shopaholic, or sabotaging ourselves in various ways, which we interpret as our personality. "It's just how I am," we might say.

So we need to take a close look at our seemingly erratic behavior, and get to the root of it, which will lead us to the abuse.

Elaborate and often terrible yet undetected abuse may be easier to see once we become parents and understand more clearly what it means to abandon a newborn child or to use our children as scapegoats. We can then identify the abuse we experienced and measure the pain we must have felt as well as the efforts we had to deploy in order not to feel it and to deny its violence. When you find yourself duplicating your parents' behavior or being tempted to do so, you realize more fully how wrong it is, what a dark place it comes from. If you resort to spanking your child, you see there is no possible justification to do so—none. You see clearly where it comes from in you and that there is no justice or good parenting in it as you had been told, or as you told yourself in order to justify your parents' bad behavior. You feel the violence it entails and you can appreciate how it is going to affect your child—so you at last know how wrong your parents were. This unlocks the pain as well as the resentment and can help to wake you up a little to your unconscious mind.

It's striking to note the number of people who start out claiming that they didn't suffer during their childhood, but who soon enough nonchalantly admit that their parents never picked them up from school, that they were left home alone for long stretches of time, or that their parents took week-long vacations, leaving them in the care of grandparents without ever calling.

Conversation is the remedy. In the kind of close conversation I engaged in, finally, with my own trusted friends and a therapist, sometimes all it took was for one of these individuals to put my feelings into words, such as "sadness" or "fear," for me to suddenly become aware of having experienced them. The process of talking through our own childhoods in this way may stun us—first because of how much it unearths but also because of how simple and straightforward the method of unearthing it can be. But it can also be such a relief, and we can find such peace in finally identifying emotions that for years have held us in their grip by remaining undetected, that have simply seemed like gaps or empty spaces or shadows. Only then we can finally make real strides toward moving on.

## Detecting Covert Abuse

But it is not always that simple—there is such a thing as covert abuse. It can be even more difficult to understand the abuse to which we were subjected if it was not perceived as such by those around us. Indeed, if we were beaten, or our parents constantly belittled us, we have objectively and recognizably been victims of abuse. It is a different story if the abuse to which we were subjected went unnoticed because our parents' behavior was considered harmless or the norm in the community in which it took place.

Consider a parent who regularly spanks or chastises their child for normal and developmentally appropriate sexual exploration, and whose discipline along these lines is considered good because of their religion. The child—and eventually the adult—will believe he is bad. It isn't difficult to imagine the long-lasting confusion this child, adolescent, and soon-to-be adult will have regarding his sexuality.

Abuse can be even more difficult to recognize, let alone acknowledge, when our parents' behavior was considered loving. For example, a father may project onto his daughter some quality unrelated to her true talents in order to please or valorize himself ("she's a genius at math," he might say, or "she's a real athlete"), disregarding the fact that this inevitably fosters feelings of inadequacy in his daughter. Confused, sensing that she didn't deserve such praise, the girl develops the painful and lasting impression that she is a fraud.

The behavior of these parents is undeniably harmful, but their abuse remains hidden because most of us don't have the tools to detect it—especially not those of us who were victims of it. Such individuals need the guidance of supportive people—such as therapists—who can define and confirm the abuse. Or they must make benchmarks for themselves that will allow them to see through their parents' apparently kind and decent behavior, in order to understand and decode the workings behind what they experienced as children, and what they continue to experience as adults and even parents. It is especially important to do so since every form of covert abuse shares the very confusing quality of hiding behind seemingly innocuous, friendly, well-intentioned and/or loving behavior.

Such is the case of Martine, who allows her son to sleep in her bed as soon as her husband, who forbids it, is away on business. Or Xavier, who takes his beautiful young daughter Sarah out as "his date" in place of his wife, who suffers from a chronic illness and is homebound.

Psychologists call this "incestuous" behavior. It implies an ambiguous relationship between parent and children, though unlike physical incest, it operates "only" on a symbolic level.

But this behavior is less trivial than it may appear. By letting him sleep in her bed, Martine gives George the symbolic place of his father, fostering an uneasy disturbance in his mind. Xavier similarly exploits Sarah by symbolically enlisting her as his wife. Even if he doesn't realize he is doing so, he is in fact proudly parading her around like a trophy because she's younger, prettier, and healthier than his wife, and Xavier thereby forces Sarah to assume the role of a significant other, thus betraying her mother. It provokes great confusion that is difficult to identify—certainly more than if she had clearly been a victim of physical incest.

Here's another similarly toxic behavior: the parent-buddy. Consider the case of Charlotte, the mother of fifteen-year-old Roxanne, one of those "cool moms" who lives a second youth through her daughter—such a common phenomenon! When organizing Roxanne's birthday parties, "Charlie" would invite more of her own friends than her daughter's, partly because the teenagers were not allowed to attend late-night events where alcohol was served. Consequently, Charlotte was lauded by her own friends for her kindness and ability to mix generations and was seen as a cool mom by Roxanne's friends. Everything seemed to be fine, though in reality Roxanne would have preferred planning her own party and celebrating it with just her friends. However, because complaining about her mother's kindness would seem ungrateful, Roxanne felt obliged to thank her mother as if she had been touched by her initiative. Yet the very opposite was true. By intruding into her world under the guise of friendliness, Charlotte put her daughter in a difficult position; Roxanne felt that she could no longer complain about her mother to her friends—in whom she should have felt able to confide—because they were so impressed by Charlotte's "coolness."

Indeed, Charlotte's desire to demonstrate that she could be a part of the same world as her daughter and show how good a mother she was masked the fact that she was actually attempting to take the role of the envied, partying teenage girl for herself. It kept Roxanne from dissociating and thus emancipating herself from her mother, and by extension, finding her way into adulthood. While seemingly harmless and even fun, the parent-buddy relationship is in reality a way for parents to control their children and not let them go.

There are other, even more subtle ways in which parents can dominate and manipulate children, such as reducing them to trophies to be shown off.

This was the case with Alexander, whose parents lived to make a spectacle of their marital bliss—the kind of marriage we may instantly recognize these days given the rise of social media. Without ever expressing it, Alexander became certain very early on that in their eyes, his greatest role and function was to admire and glorify his parents' relationship—to exist as evidence of, and to applaud and promote their image of themselves as the perfect couple.

The problem here lay first and foremost in Alexander's parents' indifference: they were so absorbed with each other, they weren't interested in the parts of him that didn't reflect on them as an amazing couple. It left him feeling miserable and lonely.

Furthermore, Alexander felt guilty for his own discomfort because he was devoted to being what his parents expected him to be. And this, in turn, made him their accomplice. He felt cowardly for letting his parents use him, even though he didn't have any choice; unless a child is old enough to live on his own, he doesn't have the option of refusing his parents' will.

Finally, Alexander felt ashamed of his duplicity. He feigned happiness in his parents' presence because he unconsciously understood that they wouldn't tolerate him having his own desires and demands, and that they would rather reject him altogether than have to get to know him. Naturally, this had a devastating effect on him.

These are good examples of what is specific to covert abuse: it provokes suffering in children that is not only undetected by those around them, but exacerbated because the children themselves take an active part in it as they allow their parents to reduce them to trophies or foils. Compounding all this, such children are continually told how lucky they are to have such united, dedicated, generous, or loving parents, as people of that kind usually do go to great lengths to appear so.

Take the example of Alice's mother, whose need to display her maternal devotion was as intense as it was unconscious. She fulfilled it at her daughter's expense by announcing to everyone that Alice was seriously ill as soon as she had a common cold, or by inventing the worst symptoms although her daughter was totally fine. She even went so far as to prolong her daughter's sicknesses by not giving Alice the right treatment for her sore throats or bronchitis.

She then kept Alice at home after duly informing everyone of her daughter's ailments, and she hysterically multiplied the number of doctors' visits in order to show off her deep, motherly devotion.

It's no wonder that once Alice reached adulthood, she struggled to understand the grievances she felt against her mother, whom everyone considered exceptionally dedicated, and to identify her mother's behavior as Munchausen syndrome by proxy.

It is impossible to conclude this overview of abuse without mentioning the most common type: neglect. Though simpler to explain than other covert forms of abuse, its effects are also easier to play down. However, it is nothing less than an everyday form of abandonment. Our children sometimes experience it in unexpected ways, such as when we don't pay attention to them because we are self-centered, engrossed in our smartphones, or under the influence of alcohol or drugs.

## Comforting Our Wounded Inner Child

Why is it indispensable for us to do this introspective work? First, to fully understand what made us suffer, and second, to rid ourselves of this pain, since it is its long-lasting nature that keeps us under the influence of our childhood. Thus, it is essential that we soothe our wounded inner child. And I know how this language might make some of us cringe. It may sound a little too hippy-dippy. A little too new age. For those of you struck by the language in this way, please keep in mind that it is about healing.

A wonderful, perhaps even the best, way to begin and achieve this process of healing is to role-play, restaging situations from our childhood that left the strongest impressions on us. We must imagine ourselves not in the role of the children we were, but in the role of our parents. Then, from an adult's perspective, we can judge whether or not our sorrow and our feelings of guilt or inadequacy are justified.

For example, imagine someone abandoned at birth who always lived with the feeling that it was her fault because she was in one way or another unable to make her parents love her. To "restage" her childhood traumatic experience, she would put herself in the place of the parents of a newborn child at the hospital faced with the decision of having to give her up. Then, this woman can ask herself whether such a parent was making the decision because the infant was guilty of something. Such an exercise can allow this woman to understand that she is by no means responsible for her parents' decision, and this would likely diminish her feelings of guilt, which ultimately wouldn't be able to survive this rational analysis.

Similarly, if we were sexually assaulted as children and no one believed or protected us at the time, we can imagine what we would do if one of our children told us that he or she had been raped or otherwise assaulted. We can then compare our parents' reaction back then to what our reaction would be today. We might see that we would unquestioningly believe our child and act accordingly by pulling them away from the aggressor and comforting them. In these exercises, it is indispensable to realize our parents' responsibility in order to confirm that we were in fact victims and to heal our own feelings of guilt.

Here is another very powerful and soothing exercise: picture yourself as the protective and benevolent parent of the child you once were. What would you do to comfort your inner child in similar situations? The mere exercise of rewriting history in this way, by saying the words we would have wanted to hear from our own parents or by imagining the behavior we think our parents should have adopted...this amounts symbolically to parenting ourselves, to doing the work of a good parent toward ourselves—a practice of wisdom and healing that can ease long-abiding pain and sadness.

# 4

# Correcting Our Behavior

*Childhood impressions do not easily fade,*
*so we'd better ensure they are good.*

—SOSTHÈNE DE LA ROCHEFOUCAULD-DOUDEAUVILLE,
*The Book of Thoughts and Maxims, 1861*

When I think back to my early years of parenting, my primary recollection is of grappling with a strong sense of guilt. First, because my interactions with my children were tainted, perhaps even contaminated, with anxiety: I was on edge, incapable of the serenity needed to attend to them, incapable of enjoying being with them. The second reason was that my anxiety didn't make me any wiser. Indeed, I could not reassure myself with the thought that my relationship with them might very well not be pleasurable and relaxed, but it was somehow productive, and I was managing to communicate maturely considered messages. I did not have sufficient control of my behavior to be consistent. In fact, in instances of my most inappropriate or irrational actions, such as upon realizing that I had been unjustifiably irritable with them, I would sometimes rationalize my behavior in my own eyes by trying, unsuccessfully, to bury deep inside me the obscure sense of having behaved unfairly and therefore having been at fault.

Or sometimes, devastated that I had so little self-control, I swore that I would monitor myself more closely and try harder, which did nothing to help me relax and proved totally ineffective because it's not about willpower!

In short, I was at an impasse and did not even realize that what made me a bad mother was not only the poor reflexes inherited from my past, but also this feeling of guilt, which shackled me and stopped me from "getting over myself" to be there for my children and think in a levelheaded way about the upbringing they needed. Unfortunately, at the time I also did not realize that until I managed to understand what was going on with me and alter my behavior—which would take some time—there was in fact a legitimate "magic tool" available to me: after lapsing back into old conditioned behavior and irritability, I could apologize to my children for my more unfair or inappropriate reactions, and explain to them in an age-appropriate way what had been going on with me when I behaved poorly. I am so happy that I finally, at one point, learned to use that magic tool. I would say to them, for example: "I am so sorry I raised my voice earlier today. It wasn't because of what you were doing, but because of my own irritation..." I discovered that apologizing did not discredit me in their eyes, nor did it compromise my parental authority—not at all. In fact, the act of apologizing and clearly telling them that I was wrong and accepted responsibility for it demonstrated intellectual and emotional honesty. Furthermore, and perhaps even more importantly, it relieved the guilt and hurt my own reactions had provoked in them—this was really very critical, as it interrupted the passing of my hurt to them, which, unstudied, they would carry around as their own hurt and later pass on to someone else, perhaps their own children. The simple act of stepping back, accepting responsibility and owning my behavior, verbally and explicitly, disrupted the cycle of harm. The act of apology gave my children an opportunity to show me that they loved me and to forgive me, which empowered them.

Equally important was the fact that by being myself and owning all my flaws, I had stopped playing a part or trying to be the perfect mother. This in turn gave my children permission to not try to become perfect children, but to accept who they were, secure in the knowledge that I too would demonstrate my love for them by forgiving them for not being perfect. As a result, our relationship became more real, more authentic.

So how do we actually change our behavior? Understanding what took place during our childhood—the abuse we may have been victim of—is not enough to prevent it from manifesting in our adult lives. Neutralizing our childhood suffering is one thing; getting rid of our ingrained tendency to repeat it is another. In order to correct this, we need to keep questioning our behavior as parents.

Let's return to the case of Isabelle, who would yell at her children whenever they started acting up in the backseat of the car. She had this attitude until the day she *examined* her response rather than dismissing it, as she usually did. Much to her surprise, this act of introspection proved comforting rather than overwhelming because it helped her make the connection between her behavior and that of her father, who acted the same way. She was then able to link her angry outbursts to her childhood and not to her own personality. Only then did she realize how much her own behavior and her refusal to confront it had made her feel guilty and anxious.

Finally relieved of the guilt that had caused her to obsess only about herself, Isabelle considered her children and decided to fight the reflex that was making them suffer. She made some time throughout the day to take mental breaks during which she would replay her behavior in her mind, like a film, to revisit her bursts of anger and consider different ways of reacting.

At first, Isabelle only became aware of her fits of rage several hours after they had occurred. But gradually, the time between her outbursts and her recognition of them got shorter and shorter. This soon allowed her to pull herself together only a few minutes after flying off the handle, and gave her enough time to devise alternatives to her behavior and apologize to her children. Then finally came the day when the moment of her awareness and recognition preceded an outburst, and she was able to totally refrain from acting out the anger; in fact, she found that she could even take pleasure in her children's noisy but endearing chatter, or entertain herself by looking for ways to calm them down.

## PUSHING OURSELVES TO BE MINDFUL

How do we become aware of our mistakes? Of course, we could question our reactions at the time they occur, or during bouts of insomnia, which we might think would be perfect times for examining our conscience. But this is rarely the case; most of us allow our everyday life to distract us from our feelings, especially when we have a sneaking suspicion that we might be bad parents, and if we feel incapable of changing ourselves. So we convince ourselves that introspection is useless, and we engage in it only when crisis or tragedy forces our hand.

What Isabelle's case reveals is that it is possible to correct inappropriate responses that stem from our childhood. At the same time, in order to succeed, it is absolutely necessary for us to be mindful about how we act toward our children. This means staying in touch with what we think and how we feel, and pushing ourselves, like Isabelle, to pause regularly throughout the day to revise our behavior, which will help us identify the mistakes we make automatically.

This deliberate and systematic effort is something we must commit to making on a permanent, regular basis regardless of our children's age, because this introspection is a fundamental part of our job as parents. It is easier said than done, as it entails confronting the evidence we have reacted poorly with our children and giving it ample space within our conscience such that we can properly examine and analyze our questionable behavior with them. More often than not, we will find that we are reproducing our own parents' hurtful behavior, which is bound to similarly upset our children in turn. It is essential that we question that damaging tendency instead of forcing it out of our minds, because avoidance only further traps us in a sense of guilt, or fear, or panic that is both painful and crippling.

## RECOGNIZING RESPONSES THAT STEM FROM OUR OWN CHILDHOOD

Still, how do we detect among all our reactions the unfortunate ones that stem from our childhood? There are several ways to do so. We can start by examining what alarms us in our behavior as well as our children's, which is most often an echo of ours. These responses can be tricky to detect, especially when they don't strike us as obviously bad, as they might when we are lashing out or acting up out of anger or frustration.

Indeed, this behavior can also manifest in a very discreet, insidious, or seemingly kind way, letting our children down. Even if it seems indulgent, such behavior may very well stem from a childhood wound. So we must also look out for seemingly accommodating behavior, such as when we let our children spend the day in front of the television because we don't want to deal with them, or when we feel a strong need to be loved and wrongly think that we will succeed by giving in to our children's every wish. Chances are that these responses stem from our childhood wounds, and may prove to be as disastrous for our children as excessive discipline would be.

It can also be hard to detect our "bad" or problematic responses that stem from our own childhood because our behavior may seem to us to be rational and legitimate. In short, we feel we are doing good!

Consider the case of Nadia, who prevented her daughter Josie, age fifteen, from joining her father on Saturday evenings when he did humanitarian work, which went on until 10 p.m. Nadia's rationale was that her daughter needed to be in bed by 9 p.m. in order to be rested for school—even though the next day was Sunday! She justified this rule by claiming that it was "for Josie's own good." But if Nadia had reflected upon this, she would have realized that her point was ill conceived, that she had resisted a closer look, and that her response was most likely an automatic reflex stemming from her own childhood that was causing her to punish Josie by controlling her or keeping her from having a close relationship with her father.

What this example shows is that we should be particularly wary of the parenting principles we adopt instinctively and strongly without any cross-examination, because what is driving them may very well be our own childhood wound(s). These unstudied principles often allow us excuses to engage in the same questionable behavior our parents did, simply adapted to the current situation—just as chameleons adapt to varying circumstances.

Take Angela, a forty-five-year-old mother who humiliated her twelve-year-old daughter, Cassie, at a restaurant. As soon as Cassie ordered dessert, Angela hailed back the waiter, demanding he bring only a half-portion, before adding sternly: "that will be more than enough." If someone had asked Angela to explain her behavior, she would have given a fallacious argument about money or diet, when in reality, paying the bill was not a problem, and Cassie was perfectly healthy and fit. Rather, Angela was probably, and unconsciously, trying to settle a score from her own childhood.

That is why it is important to question our disciplining as well, even if on its face it seems valid and beneficial.

This was the case with a parent who thought he was exemplifying good parenting when he admonished his fourteen-year-old son for asking for an iPad as a birthday present. The father asked his son, "Do you think I got an iPad at your age?" This man had every right to refuse to buy his son this gadget if, for example, he thought it was too expensive, or his son didn't deserve it, or he believed his son needed to show excellence in one field or another before expecting such a gift; in short, if he was aiming at instilling a certain set of values. But his reasoning, based only on "Why should you get that?" was nothing more than desire for revenge over his childhood hardships.

We should be aware that it's precisely such categorical sentences in the vein of "it's for your own good," "what makes you think you deserve it," or "because I love you" that serve to legitimize our most shameful unconscious feelings. All of these difficulties that we have in detecting responses that arise from our own childhood make it critical to constantly question the soundness of our conduct as parents by asking ourselves if it is effective, positive, and in accordance with our parenting goals. And this can be done by asking ourselves two very important parenting questions.

First, we have to ask ourselves: "Is my behavior good for me, or is it good for my children?" Because a characteristic common to our reactive responses rooted in our own childhood is that they have no constructive value. Second, to identify potential connections between our behavior as parents and our emotional trials as children, we should also ask ourselves: "Is my conduct being dictated by me, or by an echo of my parents?"

But there again we must always keep in mind that the connection between our parenting and our own childhood is not always easy to establish, because the lingering effects of our childhood can manifest themselves in different ways. Indeed, we can duplicate precisely our own parents' behavior in singular situations identical to those we experienced as children—situations like chastising our children for their bad grades or getting angry when we put them to bed. But we can also adopt our parents' flaws overall, such as yelling at or beating our children in any given situation, or after the slightest provocation. In addition, we may share the perverse feeling that drove our parents' behavior, such as a desire to dominate or take revenge on our children while hiding our aggression behind a façade of generosity and kindness—as Nadia did by not allowing her daughter Josephine to accompany her father on his humanitarian projects, on the pretext that the girl needed her sleep. The perversity behind this seemingly constructive logic is as difficult to detect in our own behavior as it was in our parents', as what is at stake isn't the nature of our reactions, but their hidden motives, and the true agenda behind them.

In short, the ways we project and act upon our childhood traumas may be more or less tricky to detect, and also to accept. Our responses sometimes provoke such toxic behavior that it can frighten us, overwhelm us with guilt, and keep us from getting to the bottom of our distress. The more dire the situation, the more urgent the need to seek the help of a professional. Because it is when we try to justify our behavior to a neutral interlocutor that we begin to see our ambivalences, which then become easier to untangle and move beyond.


## CHANGING OUR BEHAVIOR

### Practice Makes Perfect

It is of course crucial we modify our behavior. But since our willpower alone is of no help in tackling our unconscious mechanisms, it is necessary to undertake a rigorous examination of our behavior if we are to open our eyes to our automatic reflexes. Once uncovered and brought clearly into our consciousness, these reflexes become amenable to our efforts to effect positive change.

Like a waltz, this internal process works in three stages. We start with a period of introspection to detect our automatic reflexes, analyze how our childhood motivates and triggers them, and finally imagine alternative responses. The process requires perseverance, and practice makes perfect. After all, it is only the repetition of that internal process that allows us to get a handle on our reflexes or, at the very least, to distance ourselves from them and better understand their ability to harm our children. Doing so is a game changer, because in the worst-case scenario, if we were to beat our children, at the very least apologizing and admitting our helplessness, as well as recognizing our children's suffering, may give them the necessary tools to legitimize their feelings and understand that it isn't their fault, but ours. And it may even give them a chance to overcome our violence.

## Disobeying Our Parents

Once we establish a connection between our responses and those of our own parents, it becomes clear we need to disobey them to change our behavior, and disagree with statements such as: "You will see how hard it is when you become a parent"; "You will understand what I went through; get your turn, and then you will know that I was right, that children are annoying, difficult, and ungrateful..." Because the reason why our parents want us so badly to follow their footsteps is that they sense that if we share their views and imitate their behavior, we are showing them our approval and paying them homage. Therefore, unless our childhood was blissful, it is critical to challenge our parents' words and ideas, and to refuse their command, however implicit, to do just as they did, and just as poorly. The only constructive way to get even is to do better.

But this doesn't mean it is necessary confront our parents if we were abused. Showing appropriate behavior with our own children is a much more powerful response than openly blaming them and confronting them for their mistakes as parents. And if it matters to you, know that such a response does not go unnoticed. Our own parents usually interpret our benevolence toward our own children as a rebellion far more powerful and radical than criticism.

Even if and when we are able to refrain from repeating our own parents' wrongdoing, our work as parents is ongoing—for it is not enough to refrain from reproducing their harm. We must choose to repair harm with good, not by doing the complete opposite, as we've seen, but by doing differently with our children. For example, if our parents spent our whole childhood trying to get rid of us, we must learn to find pleasure in the company of our children rather than simply spending all our time with our children.

## Finding Alternative Behavior

For myself, I stumbled quite a bit before finding alternative ways of behaving with my children, and I believe this is pretty common. Take Isabelle, who shared with me some of the ways that, over the course of several months, she experimented with persuading her children to be quieter in the backseat. Instead of expecting obedience, she could appeal to their kindness and ask them to be less rowdy as a favor; she could otherwise get out of the car to give them five minutes to settle down before organizing a silence contest. Or resort to humor rather than anger: "I will roast you little piggies over a campfire, if you don't..."

As with Isabelle and as with me, the ability to develop alternative ways of behaving needs to be exercised like a muscle. For this to work, we first need to know what behaviors are worth putting in place of the old ones. This requires us to have an idea of what is good for our children and what is not, which becomes increasingly difficult to realize in proportion to how much our parents failed us in this regard.

In one of my favorite films, Mommy, Xavier Dolan tells the story of the conflicted but tender relationship between an overwhelmed mother and her impulsive, violent son. After the death of his father three years earlier, sixteen-year-old Steve is sent to a treatment facility for children with behavioral problems. After being found responsible for setting fire to one of the buildings, Steve is returned to his mother. Their reunion and explosive cohabitation oscillates between love, violence, and insults. Di, the immature mother who manifests a passionate love for her son despite his impulsiveness, tries to keep him with her. But she has a hard time discerning what is good for her son and what is good for her, to the point that she hesitates to push her son away when he goes as far as kissing her on the lips. Nevertheless, when he later attempts to kill himself, Di, to avoid a tragedy, decides to have him committed in the hope that he can be helped. "It's not because we love someone that we can save him. Love has nothing to do with it," states a hospital worker.

Although this story is a melodramatic and extreme parenting situation, the moral is useful to all parents. Our love for our children is not enough: we need to rely on solid criteria and benchmarks—not our own moods or impulses—to clearly and intentionally define our priorities in raising our children. And that is the subject matter of the following chapters of this book.

# PART THREE

# SETTING
# THE RECORD
# STRAIGHT

# 5

><

# The Perfect Parents
Are Imperfect

*Child rearing is to children what water is to plants.*
—SOSTHÈNE DE LA ROCHEFOUCAULD-DOUDEAUVILLE,
*Le Livre des pensées et maximes* (The Book of Thoughts
and Maxims, 1861)

## THE OBSESSION WITH PERFECTION

As Beyoncé lucidly and somewhat ironically points out in her song "Pretty Hurts," Americans are obsessed with perfection. I couldn't agree more, even if an icon such as she might in fact contribute to the obsession. The pressure assaults Americans from all sides: expectations of achieving polished, effortless perfection as partners, as children, as students, in their careers... and, of course, as parents.

Paradoxically, it seems things are made worse for parents who, like me, have read a lot of literature about parenting that emphasizes the importance of parental dedication. Because as much as the literature is accurate and useful, stressing how important parenting is, it can also paralyze us with fear. Indeed, we have internalized the fact that children need a lot of attention and that everything we do has a huge impact on them. So we live with the constant fear of making mistakes, and the only insurance we feel we have to prevent failure is to do everything by the book or, should I say, by the multitude of books, which inevitably leads us to try to be perfect on all fronts.

To top it all off, we are also bombarded with a picture-perfect image of parenting and family that is delivered to us via a never-ending stream of media in contemporary culture. This makes already anxious parents strive even harder for perfection, which ultimately puts their children's well-being at stake since, instead of focusing on their children, these parents frequently end up spending all of their time and energy checking off the "perfect parents' duties" boxes. And what lists of duties we've developed! In contemporary American culture, such a list can even include cooking home-made meals from scratch and photographing and sharing them with the world (or at least with one's closest circle of hundreds of competing parents); in some cases in America, *homesteading* has become the latest bar by which to measure parental dedication. If you're not already familiar with it, search social media for beautifully decorated homeschool classrooms, pantries filled with home-grown, masterfully preserved fruits and vegetables, and mommy fashion blogs on the side to generate extra income.

*Tully* is a 2018 film directed by Jason Reitman and starring Charlize Theron. The film is a sharply funny interrogation of the deteriorating self-esteem and even mental health of a woman under immense parental and domestic pressure. Theron plays Marlo, who unexpectedly gives birth to an unplanned third child at forty. Her rich brother

(Mark Duplass) offers a night nurse, as a celebratory gift, to help Marlo manage the early days. At first, Marlo is offended by the suggestion that she needs help and can't handle everything on her own. Eventually, she relents and invites the night nurse, Tully (played by Mackenzie Davis), into her home. Tully is a twenty-six-year-old sexy American version of Mary Poppins who embodies everything it is too late for Marlo to be.

Lest I spoil an edgy film with an unexpected twist that I really do encourage parents to watch for themselves, I'll just say this: eventually, Marlo learns that parenting happily means being vulnerable. Trying to be Wonder Woman leads not to domestic and marital bliss or social media stardom, but to mind-breaking depression and exhaustion. The pursuit of parental perfection drives us to feel endlessly inadequate, guilty, and miserable. We say we know this, we acknowledge how true it is…yet so many American parents, and mothers in particular (albeit not exclusively), are under the spell of cultural pressure and marketing influences attempting to define them.

This quest for perfection, which inevitably leads us to ignore our own needs (and in many cases, our children's needs), or to give up our passions, is not a good lesson to our children, who will then believe that self-sacrifice is the way to be a "good" person and will contribute in turn to the vicious cycle of "bad" parenting.

Finally, striving to be perfect and happy doesn't work. We will never be the former, and, while we keep trying and trying, we can never fully be the latter. Indeed, this quest for perfection only leads us to pretend to be perfect in the hope of becoming so. And this is very confusing and toxic, since it triggers self-consciousness and guilt, which then trap us inside our imperfections and insecurities. But this behavior is not good for our children either, notably because our being seemingly perfect doesn't give them the chance to know who we truly are, and it puts them in a situation where growing up, learning, and making mistakes makes them feel, in comparison, disappointingly imperfect.

## THE IMPERFECT PARENTS

The good news is that the perfect parents are imperfect. In fact, there is no such thing as a perfect parent, as the well-known psychologist D.W. Winnicott (1896–1971) acknowledged when he invented the concept of the "good enough" parent, which was then picked up and carried further by writer and cultural critic Bruno Bettelheim (1903–1990). But we act as if we had forgotten all about them and the fact that we can only be the best parents we can hope to be.

Now take a deep breath and see if you can feel what a relief this is. What this means in our contemporary culture is that the best parents are human and deal with reality as it unfolds, one day at a time. Parenting is not a role, a hologram, or a job description into which our real personality is meant to vanish. So let's not hide our constraints behind a picture-perfect image of parents and let's be true to ourselves and to our children. What defines a parent/individual may be a deeply personal matter, but we can agree that it is not perfection.

If it is not being perfect, what, as parents, are we fundamentally supposed to *do*? To a greater extent than we'd like to admit, we don't really even know. The debates we engage in are mostly monopolized by and limited to practical questions, such as how much time we spend with our children, our degree of involvement in their education, and the activities we participate in with them.

But what about the emotional aspect of parenting? What would be best for our children? We think we can rely on our unconditional love to help them develop. But we cannot expect ourselves to feel and demonstrate our love, even if it is indeed unconditional, 24/7 and 100 percent of the time.

Yet while we are focusing only on our love for our children, we downplay or ignore altogether how utterly critical it is to simply feel the joy of being with them.

## THE BEST PARENTS THRIVE IN THEIR CHILDREN'S COMPANY

If only someone had told me that enjoying being with my children was one of my most important parental "duties"! Concerned as I was with doing the opposite of my parents, who belonged to a generation in France that spent little or no time with their children, I threw myself wholeheartedly into what many perceive to be a very American dynamic, which entails devoting yourself body and soul to your children, and leaving little or no time and space for yourself as an adult.

Instead of thinking about my relationship with each one of my children, I put most of my focus on what I thought I was supposed to do, and how much: how much time I spent, how many activities, my daily to-do list, cooking meals, giving baths, overseeing homework. In other words, I was so obsessed with being a good mother that I wasn't thinking about the best way to help my children develop. And I know I'm not alone in that case.

Of course, I had been bitten by the perfection bug. But I also had no idea how to interact with my children as I had never experienced closeness with my own parents. In turn, parenting was bringing me no joy. This made me feel inadequate, and even disabled, but I never thought I should try to change the situation because I didn't think it mattered much. I felt it was a shame for me not to experience such joy, but I was convinced that this would have no impact on my children, because they had the full benefit of what really mattered: my love and just my being there in the first place. I could not have been more wrong.

Indeed, I accomplished these tasks with a rigor that left my children no room to express themselves or develop a relationship with me that should have been mutual rather than a one-way street, directed by me. Moreover, even though my children did not consciously acknowledge it, they could tell when I was putting on an act, when I was bored, for example (after all, I wasn't really engaged because I was artificially trying to embody unconditional love), and they sometimes had clear proof of it when they caught me yawning at the park or closing my eyes during one of their school performances or after-school programs. The net result was that they often felt alone even when I was physically there with them.

It takes only a small step for them to get from there to believing they were responsible for my boredom and, therefore, must have been inadequate or somehow unworthy, and it is a step they inevitably took, as all children are quick to feel responsible for everything. This is why I should have thought about my enjoyment of motherhood, should have been amazed I felt none, and should have refused to let the situation persist, because this predicament would have more harmful consequences than I could imagine, and made me waste a lot of time and lose out on much happiness with my children.

So, heartbreaking or peculiar as it might sound, it may be necessary for parents to actually learn to enjoy their children's company. This is especially true if they didn't have a warm, loving relationship with their own parents, because they cannot draw from their childhood experience to know how to love their children. In this case, for such parents to feel this joy, they have to mentally put aside their fatigue and reflect upon what they do or don't like to do with their baby. Do they like to go on walks, give the baby its bath, sing songs? Do they not like changing diapers, going to the playground, or feeding the baby? Whichever activities they most enjoy should be the ones they commit to pursuing as much as possible. For example, if a mother likes bathing her child but it is something normally done by the babysitter while the mother's at the office, she should set her schedule accordingly so that she's able to bathe her child once she's home from work instead. Priority must be given to these moments of pleasure, even if it means giving the baby two baths a day, because once the mother's desire is experienced and expressed, her pleasure will grow.

By now it has been well established that spending all our time with our children is less important than enjoying the time we spend with them. Indeed, it is crucial for children to perceive that they bring joy to their parents because they will draw from it the feeling of being a blessing, a gift, a wonder in their eyes. This will build their self-confidence, whereas they will have the impression that they are worthless if they feel they are a source of stress, fatigue, or boredom.

This further supports the notion that those of us who no longer get along with our spouses should divorce rather than stay together "for the sake" of our children, who in the latter scenario would effectively become responsible for our misery. It is thus imperative that we never allow ourselves to blame our life choices on our children or to make them responsible for our hardships, because it is an unfair and untenable burden for children to shoulder, and its negative impact can last well into adulthood. In such cases, once they are grown-ups, they may be left with the feeling of being toxic.

Take the case of Bob, a handsome thirty-five-year-old heterosexual man who couldn't commit to a woman because he was convinced he would make her suffer. After consulting a psychologist, Bob explained that his mother never got to finish her Ph.D. in philosophy—her lifelong dream—because of him. His therapist responded, "What do you mean 'because of you'? She could have gone back to school at any point after your birth, right? Then it isn't your fault. She used you as an excuse, which made you feel responsible for her failure—a burden you still carry with you today."

This residual scar may alternatively lead children to reproduce the same behavior as their parents.

This was the observation made by Linda, a young married woman who fell in love with Thomas, also married, who used to tell her how much he suffered as a child because his parents constantly repeated that they didn't want to separate because of their children—which caused Thomas to feel responsible for their unhappiness. Linda decided to divorce her husband to be with Thomas, since he was as much in love with her as she was with him. But once Linda did, Thomas changed his mind using the same argument: "I can't divorce because of my children." In truth, happy children are children who bring happiness to their parents, because this gives them the certainty of being worthy of love.

## THE BEST PARENTS MAKE THEIR CHILDREN THEIR NUMBER-ONE PRIORITY

Examining the difference between parenting styles in France and the US can be quite instructive. Until the very recent arrival of a new generation of American-style, very hands-on parenting, the prevailing trend in France was reluctance to make child-rearing a priority. Too much dedication had a bad reputation. It introduced the dangers of altering the balance of the parents' relationship, of living an embarrassingly conspicuous "bourgeois" life, and/or of relinquishing every other aspect of one's adult life. In France, these dangers amounted to a parental refusal to make radical life changes for the sake of a child or children, and this is actually feasible in a country where early childcare is mostly subsidized, and where it is easy and quite inexpensive to entrust children to daycare, government-licensed childcare providers, or even to family members who live nearby.

Add to this that the French are a discreet nation, not given to effusiveness, and many loving parents are reluctant to express or sometimes even acknowledge their love and affection for their children, but instead complain directly or indirectly about them, citing how exhausting they are or how little time they have for themselves.

This sort of behavior and narrative would be frowned upon in the US, where, as we saw, social pressure to behave like model parents is so strong that no parent would dare say he or she is ever bored by parenting, and where, in any event, child care is so expensive and difficult to find that there are scant options open to parents other than devoting themselves all day every day to raising their children. But this devotion almost inevitably turns into helicopter parenting. If you think about it, though, given that so-called soccer moms are expected to live their children's lives rather than their own, how could anyone criticize them for being overinvolved and wanting their children to be champions?

So while today's advice in France often warns parents against neglecting their own emotional, professional, or cultural lives when raising their children, mainstream

American culture believes the opposite—yet neither cultural message seems quite right! Despite this confusion, the fact remains that whether we are surrounded by over-involved or under-involved parents, it is critical that we make our children our number-one priority.

Indeed, being seriously involved in our children's up-bringing is a moral imperative, since, as we saw previously, the more we pay attention to our children, the better they develop. Conversely, the less we care for our children, the more trouble they are going to have, both as children and as adults.

If, when they are young, children usually don't allow themselves to demonstrate their suffering because of the vulnerability and dependence inherent in early childhood, they will make up for it as soon as they grow up and find ways to do so, starting in adolescence. For instance, they may hurt themselves or others, exemplifying the old saying, "Small children, small problems. Big children, big problems." And as easy as it is to raise five-year-old children—teaching them respect and values by correcting their silly, small mistakes on a daily basis—it is difficult to start disciplining them when they are teenagers and their mistakes could lead them to drugs, theft, or self-mutilation. Metaphorically speaking, if we don't lift up and carry our children when they are little, we run the risk of having to do so when they are older and a lot heavier.

Ideally, our involvement with our children is a lot less demanding when they are older than in their early years. Teenagers who have assimilated the values that we have instilled in them at a young age require only benevolent supervision, not incessant control. In short, raising children requires an effort that decreases over time. To put it in numerical terms, consider that parenting should take, say, 80 percent of our time when children are born, 60 percent at age three, 40 percent at age twelve, and 10 percent at age seventeen. Otherwise, there may be a severe price to pay when children turn twenty, drop out, have eating disorders, become drug addicts or delinquents, and turn the work of parenting into an effort worth 3,000 percent of our time.

But making our children our number-one priority is also a pragmatic imperative, as it is the best way for us to ensure our children gain independence. Indeed, children who receive a loving and devoted upbringing for the first twenty years of their lives will have their fill of parental love and attention. They won't really need their parents after that, and will be able to leave the nest with complete serenity. This is the very definition of independence, and it fosters a wonderful relationship between adult children and their parents, even if we may, as parents tend to, continue to care and worry about our daughters and sons. On the other hand, children who lacked attention and love will spend their whole lives circling back to their parents in search of what was missing during those early formative years of life.

Nevertheless, we're surrounded by endless examples of the alternative approach: think of the number of distressed parents whose children struggle to find their bearings, and make their parents pay for the errors they made during their unhappy childhoods. Also consider the amount of time these parents devote to trying to fix their children's mistakes, or support them because they are incapable of taking care of themselves, and all the energy spent trying to mend their strained relationship.

## THE BEST PARENTS CONFRONT THEIR OWN ISSUES AND FEARS

Making our children our number-one priority raises fears and reluctance that we need to address in order to parent from an authentic place and to take pleasure while doing so.

### The Fear of Compromising Their Love Life

One of our first sources of anxiety connected to child-rearing surfaces even before our children are born: we worry that once they come into our lives, we will no longer have enough love or energy for our partner. But in truth, there is no need to worry about the limits of our capacity for love. Indeed, a similar fear arises with the birth of each new child: "Will I be able to love this child as much as my firstborn? Do I have enough love for two, three, or four children?" And yet this fear dissipates the same way every time, as we come to understand that our ability to love is inexhaustible, and that we don't need to cut back on how much we love our partner or other children in order to love our newborn.

That said, the birth of a child might alter or destroy the equilibrium in our relationship with our partner. For example, one spouse may fear the other will abandon them emotionally or sexually for the newborn's benefit.

Especially early on, it may sound unimaginable, but to counteract this worry, new parents should make love with their partners as often as possible after they give birth, if not as frequently as before. It is a mistake to stop having sex, or to have it less often, as soon as we are tired. After all, far from being tiring, having sex is relaxing, notably thanks to the release of endorphins. In addition, sex fosters a kind of powerful nonverbal communication that answers questions such as: "Do you love me? Do you still think I'm attractive? Do you love me less than our child?" and in the end, having discussions along these lines turns out to be much more exhausting than enjoying a bit of affectionate physical contact. Therefore, new parents should help their tired spouse to regain their sex drive by resuming their role as romantic partners as soon as possible. This is more beneficial because, for example, by distracting the new mother from her child in order to protect their privacy as a couple, the father prevents the child from becoming the mother's sole focus, thereby sparing the child the heavy burden of feeling entirely responsible for his or her mother's well-being.

By the same token, even though our involvement as parents in no way implies any abandonment of our significant other, who may be fearing just that, it does undeniably cause a shift within our relationship.

Here's another example of the fear of compromising our relationship with our partner, in this case manifesting as frustration and concern for a young father, Frank, who was feeling destabilized and unsure of his place when his wife, overflowing with hormones and powerful feelings, was often literally attached to their newborn.

He lamented to his therapist, "I don't understand my wife. Before our child's birth, she refused to wake up at night to have sex or to make me something to eat if I was hungry, for example. But now, she gets up as soon as the baby cries." In other words, she does for their child what she never did for him, which Frank took as a sign of favoritism toward the child. His therapist had to explain that Frank's wife hadn't changed, that she still wanted to sleep through the night, but that she had to get up for their child when he would cry because he wasn't able to take care of himself. Doing so could be vital, especially if the child had a fever, threw up, or faced any risk of sudden infant death syndrome. Whereas if he, Frank, got hungry at night, it wasn't absolutely necessary for her to get up since he was not in danger and could cook his own pasta.

A child's arrival may require a readjustment within our relationship with our partner. But isn't it the same with a move, a new job, or different work schedules? In those instances, too, our mood and our time with our significant other can also undergo some modification. In fact, life itself demands of all people, including those who are in a relationship, a permanent readjustment as conditions change. And there is no reason to expect anything different from the arrival of a child.

But it isn't always so simple. For instance, a child definitely presents a disruption to relationships in which one spouse parents the other. In such cases, the real child implicitly calls the behavior of the symbolic child into question. This person may quite likely reject the idea of getting involved in raising the child, or hinder the partner who is trying to raise their child.

Such was the case with Diane, who suddenly couldn't stand her husband Ken's childish behavior even though she had tolerated and at times even encouraged it to satisfy her mothering instincts before the birth of their daughter. Up until then, Diane called Ken "my baby" and did everything for him, anticipating his every desire without ever asking for anything in return. In short, she did for him all the things a baby needs but a husband shouldn't—or at least not to such a degree. While it is not a problem to baby our significant other some of the time, catering to them 24/7 is bound to lead to dysfunction, for although we all need to feel cared for in our relationship, we also don't want to feel as though our partner needs us as a caregiver or an alter ego.

Unsurprisingly, Ken didn't respond well to his wife's changed behavior. Diane found it unnecessary for her husband to be responsible and protective when she was childless, because she felt independent, self-reliant, and sure of herself; after having the baby, she suddenly did want him to be that reassuring figure, amid her newfound vulnerabilities and insecurities.

And it was unfair of Diane to resent her husband since she hadn't been consistent in her demands. Ken would probably have been perfectly capable of being protective of her had she always shown signs of vulnerability or helplessness, and simply asked him for more help and support after the birth of their daughter.

Indeed, what matters most in our relationship with our partner is not the distribution of roles, which are interchangeable and can go from traditional to nontraditional and back again. (This holds true for many same-sex couples or arrangements in which the wife changes the tire and the husband gives the baby their bottle.) No, the important thing is for us to give some thought to our roles from the beginning and to not take on roles that we cannot sustain over time, such as we've seen with the spouse who is treated like a baby—an arrangement that can last only as long as there is no real baby in the house.

Our hesitation to engage fully and honestly in parenting can also affect our relationships if we don't view family life in the same way as our partner does. An example is one parent being less enthusiastic about raising children in the first place. This is what happened to Natalie, who could only convince Alan that they should have a child by offering to manage everything so as to maintain their lifestyle. To keep her promise, Natalie had to minimize the havoc caused by the birth of their daughter Ella so that Alan wouldn't come to resent the little girl. Afterward, in trying to take care of Ella without disrupting her marriage, Natalie quickly got in the habit of relying on daycare, babysitters, and grandparents. In short, Natalie exhausted herself by hiding her fatigue from Alan, her difficulties and her worries as a mother, so as to keep her parental role from weighing on their relationship and daily life. Instead, she projected the image of the young, available, and carefree woman she was before Ella's birth, which notably meant having dinners with friends, going to the movies on weekends, and so forth. In other words, Natalie tried to do it all with no apparent effort while masking her involvement and role as a parent. However, by spreading herself so thin by trying to maintain two lives, Natalie ended up losing on both fronts. She lost the feeling of pleasure she found in her former life, especially the happiness she felt with Alan, and she was unable to take pleasure in taking care of her daughter. The strain was destroying both her marriage and her relationship with her daughter.

You may wonder how any of this applies to you if you're a single parent. The fundamental point is the same: if not sex and maintaining a good marriage with your spouse, it is still critical for your health and the health of your child that you have someone or something pulling you out of an "absolute" relation with your kids. You cannot be in an exclusive and passionate relationship with no one but your children. It is too much for a child to be responsible for his or her parents' happiness and fulfillment in this way.

Take my friend Evie, a single parent of a toddler and baby. She believed her children had to make her happy because they were the only people in her life—the only thing at all. She had no hobbies, no friends, no books, no activities other than child-rearing and perhaps watching television. The bond between Evie and her two children was as tight as could be, but they sensed the responsibility this bond put upon them. Eventually they began to resent Evie's presence in their lives, around the same time she began to realize how totally dependent she had become on them, and how crushing a load that was for them.

## Reluctance to Change Their Lifestyle

I have lived extensively in France and in the US, two countries with, as I have said, very different—even opposed—parenting philosophies.

As I see it, French parents are reluctant to change their lifestyle. One reason for this may be that they easily get turned off by the image of the stereotypical nuclear family that revolves entirely around children, planning, routine, sippy cups, and car seats. Many of them could also be under the spell of today's obsession with eternal youth, and want to keep "going with the flow," improvising their lives the way teenagers do, without the responsibilities and serious anxieties that come along with the work of parenting.

This is a much more pernicious attitude than it appears; by refusing to make sacrifices and behaving as if they had no children, they then unfortunately raise children who end up, in turn, behaving as if they had no parents, and suffer, are delinquent, or harm themselves as a result. Several arguments can be made to restrain or eradicate such an inclination to be selfish parents, some of which may seem contradictory at face value.

First, raising children has an undeniable downside: the end of insouciant living. Indeed, whatever the support made available to us, whether from relatives or caretakers, the time of responsibility only for ourselves is over once we become parents. We are no longer alone, and this radical change brings with it a number of duties. We no longer have the right to put ourselves in dangerous situations. We no longer have the right to behave badly, to set the wrong example, nor can we afford to be financially irresponsible since we have to provide for our children.

But instead of focusing on this apparent downside, we can accept, applaud, and honor the act of devoting ourselves to our children. We can remember that raising children—rather than forcing us to give up or give in, choosing conformity and tradition at the expense of creativity, imagination, and innovation—is a lifelong, life-changing project, an adventure essential to humankind, and too demanding to be done using half measures.

Second, being a parent is similar to playing a sport at a professional level; it requires years of effort before reaching the desired result. Therefore, far from being boring and conventional, it implies and requires the dedication and self-sacrifice that brings us, as all adventures do, the greatest possible satisfaction—vastly superior to enjoying ourselves by going to a movie theater, for example. This fact ought to lead us to take our responsibilities seriously and fulfill our role completely, even at the expense of all the other paths we may have considered following in our lives. Just as an adventurer embarking on a sailing trip around the world would have to write off dinners with friends or partying, so must we. Accepting our new obligations does not make us uncool or conventional.

Most of this doesn't apply to the US parenting philosophy. Indeed, in the US, it seems like a "good" mother must take something akin to the holy orders of parenting. She must "do it all"—as much from necessity as from cultural myth. She'll either wrap her baby and carry her on her back or chest for a full year, breastfeeding up to age four, even homeschooling, or she will drop her three-month-old infant off at daycare, compensating for the guilt and neglect by driving her growing children from lesson to lesson (karate, dance, swimming, soccer) in her "free" time after work and on weekends until the child is off in college.

It may seem like these latter stereotypes about parents who are all too happy to change their lifestyles are limited to Americans, and that it is only the French who are allergic to giving up adult social life. But in both countries, it appears to be increasingly "cool" to *look* like you're parenting, and parenting well, effortlessly, and beautifully. Perhaps due to the rise of social media, children have become the ultimate accessory, especially among celebrities who bring them to fashion shows, onto the red carpet, on yachts... And let's not forget the super moms who homeschool, run their businesses from home, and are also masters at crafting, baking, blogging, and so forth.

Again, where is the joy in parenting in all this? It should be the real motivation to change our lifestyle. Yet it seems no greater consideration is given to the pleasure of parenting in either country, but for very different—even seemingly opposite—reasons. It is difficult for American parents to find the time and energy to experience the joy of being with their children when, for example, many have responded to cultural pressure by overcommitting their children to academics, clubs, and sports. Moreover, given the reality of both parents having to work full time and paying totally unreasonable amounts of money for childcare, raising children can be an exhausting trap that is almost impossible to escape. But it is equally difficult in France where social pressure often discourages parents who let themselves be defined by parenting, as if parents who want to engage fully in parenting were failing at being complete sophisticated adults.

## The Fear of Giving Up Their Personal Life

We may also fear that devoting ourselves wholeheartedly to raising our children entails giving up all other aspects of our lives; this concern is especially relevant to mothers who are already forced to put their lives and careers on hold to give birth and, in the US, to parents who are forced to put even beloved careers on hold because of the exorbitant cost of childcare. The extent to which a new parent has to abandon their career, for example, is a question of privilege, yes—but making your new child a priority does not require that you sacrifice everything that had been formerly meaningful and important to you, whatever your income, and whichever country you call home.

While socioeconomic realities of raising children in the US, at least, can prove incredibly challenging, it is important for the health of both parents and children that, to the greatest extent possible, you do not sacrifice your love of work or your other interests. Doing so can foster resentment between the parents, and between each parent and their children.

Tom, for example, loved hunting; when he had his first child, he told his therapist, "My hunting days are over! Since the birth of my baby, I can't picture bringing my wife along every Sunday as I did before." His therapist disagreed, advising him: "If you stop, you will resent your wife and your child, and I'll see you back in two years to discuss divorce. Keep hunting, not every weekend, but maybe every three weeks."

In sum, devoting ourselves to raising our children does not mean giving up what matters to us—especially if we are devoted to raising healthy, well-adjusted children. But this entails that we really try to reconcile all aspects of our lives, without giving in to the common temptation of using our children as an excuse to nag our partner, prolong a dysfunctional relationship, or stop working and abandon our own personal growth.

This was the case with Betty, who gave up working when her fourth child, Julia—whom she referred to as an "accident"—was born. Three years later, the stay-at-home mom was endlessly complaining about her daughter, who was crying nonstop and uncontrollable. (Julia was not the reason why Betty began seeing a therapist, with whom she barely spoke about the little girl.) However, Betty complained about Julia even after the child started attending school. Regardless of all the hours Julia wasn't around, Betty could not find time for herself because of her anxiety over her daughter's kicking and screaming tantrums. Betty's therapist then started inquiring about Betty's professional life and found out that Julia, the so-called accident child, was at least in part a perfect alibi for Betty to quit a job she had no substantial interest in. From then on, Betty confided that in truth she had always wanted to become an architect but never gave the degree a chance. Past the age of forty, she couldn't bring herself to go back to school, especially in such a difficult field. Finally, thanks to her therapist, Betty came to realize that, rather than being a priority, Julia was her unconscious justification for giving up her career dreams without having to face her own fears, and that she had turned her daughter into a little monster simply to account for her own life choices.

It also may happen that we use our teenage child as a reason to live, or to save a dying relationship that could only survive or mend itself at the expense of our "problem child."

Such was the situation in which Oscar found himself. Although he constantly argued with his wife, Liz, he refused to consider ending their marriage and kept going "for the sake" of their drug-addicted son. As soon as the son's addiction surfaced, it consumed all of Oscar and Liz's time and energy. Although it was not enough to put their marriage back together again, it did give them a common topic of conversation. In a way, their son had unknowingly become their couples therapist. And when Oscar's real therapist said to him, "Your problem is your marriage; do you think you and your wife could possibly be over?" he replied, "Maybe, but what do I do about my son?" He didn't understand that his tenacious grip on his marriage, despite his incompatibility with his wife, was a root cause of his son's affliction. His son in turn felt he couldn't confide in either of his parents without implicitly siding with one or the other in their ongoing marital war.

Or perhaps, like many friends of mine, in response to fear about "losing time" to raising your children, you and your partner resolve to divide all parenting tasks fifty-fifty. This is an unreasonable situation if it doesn't really mirror the day-to-day dynamic and responsibility allocation you had maintained in your relationship before having a baby.

The involvement of each parent often takes different forms. It is indisputably reasonable to ask our partner for help in raising our children, and indeed, there is a greater expectation of reciprocity within relationships today than there used to be; however, in a healthy family (even if the parents do not cohabitate), each parent should be able to choose the role he or she wants to play as a parent according to his or her aptitudes and personality. Ideally, tasks are entrusted to the person best suited to take them on. In traditional families, it may be that this results in the father being the one to carry children, play catch, or teach them how to ride a bike, and it is the mother who gets up in the middle of the night, which she may have to do anyway if she is breastfeeding. But everyone and every family is different, and it is important to discuss and consider carefully what the childcare priorities are, and who is best suited to the task. Raising a child or children is a long-term project, and over the years there will be plenty of time and plenty of work to ensure that each parent has taken up their share of the responsibilities.

## Not Having Enough "Me Time"

"I no longer have time for myself" is a common and recurring complaint among parents who fully engage in their children's upbringing. But are children really the only ones taking up all of our time? It's also true of our friendships, our love life, and our work. Life takes time. So why blame this on our children? Why should they always be the ones responsible for our lack of me time? In reality, this feeling is often due not to our children, but to pressure at work or tensions with our partner. We prefer to put the blame on the children because they are the newest factor, and because it's a lot easier and a lot less risky than pointing the finger at our spouse or occupation. So it's our children who unfairly take the rap. Consequently, new mothers or primary caregivers who say, "I can't take it anymore, I'm exhausted," should always begin by asking themselves how things are with their spouse or at work, because the root cause of their frustration is often there. Otherwise, it may be linked to similar constraints that they painfully experienced during childhood.

This was the case for Sandy, a mother who had a full-time nanny, but nevertheless complained that her children were taking up all of her time. Sandy eventually realized that throughout her childhood, she was burdened with the responsibility of caring for her siblings, and the feelings she experienced toward her own children were only an extension of this earlier obligation. As soon as Sandy made that connection, she was able to feel pleasure in the company of her children.

For all of these reasons, we would do well to rethink the notion of "me time" by understanding that everything we do with and for the people we love, whether it be our children, spouse, or friend, is also "me time." It contributes to our overall happiness, and anyway, we are the ones who have chosen our company. It would not be unreasonable to limit ourselves to, say, 5 percent of what we commonly label as "me time," whether shopping, hanging out with friends, getting a massage, or playing sports, in order to be with our children as often as possible, so we are truly available and there for them.

### Exhaustion

That said, the feeling of not having enough me time is based on an undeniable truth: taking care of children is exhausting. While most of us anticipate this fact, it may still take us by surprise when we first bring our newborn home from the hospital and realize that he or she requires way more time and attention than a full-time job, or when our children grow up and constantly "bug" us, asking questions and demanding attention, or later, when we must confront teenage crises.

Nevertheless, we should be careful with labeling our emotional or physical states as "exhausting"; is it really exhaustion we are feeling? Physical exhaustion is amplified by anxiety, so it's often the anxiety and not the physical exhaustion that tires us. Just look at nannies and babysitters—they don't feel the same kind or degree of fatigue because they're not as emotionally invested as we parents are.

To address this issue, it's very important for parents, and especially for primary caregivers, to get together with friends with whom we can talk and exchange ideas. We teach one another to be better parents through advice and assurances such as, "My daughter started walking at fifteen months, so you shouldn't worry that your ten-month-old son is still not walking." Although this kind of exchange won't actually diminish our load, it changes the way we experience parenting. This kind of exchange is especially important to mothers, who, even in this day and age, persist as the usual primary caregivers. Many cultures still fail to appreciate the incredibly important and demanding task of raising children, and many persist in making the mistake of assuming that caregiving is easy—for example, for women who are stay-at-home moms. They believe that it brings women automatic joy and stems from a maternal instinct, only because most mothers, for example, seem to perform effortlessly tender and loving gestures toward their children (which in truth requires harnessing heroic patience). This is why primary caregivers often feel, and rightfully so, that no one realizes the herculean efforts that parenting entails on a daily basis. It is very important that family members, loved ones, and partners also address this reality by comforting new parents, especially the primary caregivers, and by encouraging, thanking, and praising them.

### Complaining

While exhaustion is one thing, complaining about not having enough "me time" is another—and there is a quite mundane yet fascinating question at the root of these complaints: Why do we resent our children for the fact that we have to take care of them? Why make it a negative reality? After all, having children today is a choice in the majority of cases. More often than not, we wanted to have children, sometimes more than anything in the world, and many of us may have even chosen when to have them. And if our children were to be taken away from us, it would not be a relief but an irreparable loss. So why do we complain about the time they take from us, knowing that, far from being difficult or tyrannical when they require our time and attention, they purely and simply need it?

To put it another way: when we decide to go to the hairdresser, we don't complain about getting our hair shampooed, because we know that's what happens at the hairdresser. By the same token, to go back to the image of the around-the-world sailing adventurer, it would never occur to us to resent the ocean for making us stay at the helm even if it's hard and exhausting. Though we may tire and long for respite, a walk on solid ground, there remains for such adventurers a tenacious, spirited drive out on the water.

All of this just to point out that, if we have children, it is to take care of them, not to perpetually complain about what a hard job it is. Besides, there is absolutely no reason for exhaustion to stifle pleasure. Playing sports is exhausting as well, but isn't it pleasurable too? The same goes for traveling, which is as tiring as it is rewarding. When we think about it, aren't all true pleasures exhausting? Pointing the finger at our children is dodging the fact that we are unable to conceive of or experience parenting as a pleasurable activity because the sensation of fatigue is strong enough to block the very concept.

But okay, let's face it: sometimes, we *are* exhausted, and we just want peace and quiet. And this is fair, but only to a certain extent. Let's say we allow ourselves to use 30 percent of our time to relax after devoting 70 percent to our children. We must then own up to this and be up front about it without trying to make our children believe it's for their own good.

## THE BEST PARENTS ARE STRAIGHTFORWARD WITH THEIR CHILDREN

Being up front with our children only has upsides. So we should always be up front with our children—not only when we are exhausted. For example, it is imperative that we tell our children if we can't take care of them during their school vacation and thus have to send them to camp or stay at home. Or that we don't have enough money to give them private lessons, so they will have to settle for group classes instead. Indeed, by doing so, we are helping them to understand the so-called realities of life. In explaining our situation to them frankly, we are demonstrating that we value and trust them.

Moreover, treating them as valid interlocutors will give our children a sense of pride. By accepting without complaint the childcare helpers we have chosen for them, they will be contributing to the family in a positive way. What a different experience of the realities of life such children will have, versus those whose parents simply insist out of anger or shame or frustration that "this is how it's going to be, don't argue with me."

Exchanges in which we are being up front with our children give them a real chance to live a true and authentic bond with us, and to understand that fundamentally, life and love are about carrying on together amid the details and hardships of reality.

Last but not least, being real or up front usually leads to good parenting. I wish I had understood that as a young mother. I probably could have if I had taken a closer look at my friend Genevieve. She was very impatient and couldn't bear to let her children act out, especially during dinner parties or in restaurants. Being true to herself and her feelings led her to allow herself to be firm and convincing with her children when they attempted to be unruly. Her demand was so real and authentic that her children consented right away. And she never experienced what the rest of us parents do when we tiptoe around our impatience in the name of being perfect, which leads us to be torn between our desire to be a good host and to be a good and kind parent, as well as our desire to get our unruly children to stop misbehaving. We will usually fail on every count! The key to good parenting may very well be to let go of the unreasonable expectations we have for ourselves as parents. The key is to be real.

It took me a long time to understand and accept this. Unlike my friend Genevieve, I was filled with guilt for far too long. I didn't realize that engaging fully in my children's development didn't mean attempting to be an utterly dedicated perfect "American" parent—which I was doing even as a French mom—but parenting from a real and honest place.

# 6

⌖

# More Isn't Better

*The perfect is the enemy of the good.*
—*Proverb*

A s we have seen, a cultural obsession with perfection is a condition that is also reflected in parenting. On top of it all, misconceptions about unconditional love being the greatest and only necessary ingredient to good child-rearing makes for an unhelpful and even harmful belief: more is better. The more we do for our children, the happier and the more fulfilled they will become. As a result, we end up choosing quantity over quality, and taking on too much in terms of time, supervision, after school programs, and care.

## THE TIME WE DEVOTE TO OUR CHILDREN

The message that children need to feel loved and understood can lead many of us to think we ought to spend all of our time with our kids, which is not only a bad idea, it's impossible anyway. Having said that, it isn't enough for us to dispense with the notion of time together, and just tell them how much they mean to us; our love does need to be demonstrated. The widespread idea that it is best to focus on the quality rather than the quantity of time spent with them is a good rule of thumb; however, useful as the idea may be, it requires some clarification and fine-tuning.

Indeed, whether in France or the US, in our children's minds, the time we devote to them is indicative of our interest in them. It is therefore essential to spend enough quality time with them to clearly convey how important they are to us. It is no use for us to tell them so if our behavior proves otherwise. And a child's response to this sort of disparity would make perfect sense. Imagine that your partner praises your fantastic sense of direction, but never asks for your advice when trying to find his or her way around, or always goes the opposite direction from the one you suggest. You would understandably start to think your significant other doesn't trust you, and you might even begin to doubt your sense of direction. Indeed, our behavior always speaks more forcefully than our words. Our children thus infer how important they are from our behavior and then draw conclusions about their own value—feelings that turn out to be crucial in determining how our children ultimately take care of themselves, especially during adolescence. If they feel valued, they will avoid harmful behavior, or will at least give themselves a chance to get out of a risky situation.

So, those of us who do not take the time to watch, listen, and understand our children are putting them at great risk; if their thoughts and emotions are not taken into account, they will likely stifle them to the point of numbness, thereby losing a valuable compass for balance and success.

Consider Toby, age fifteen, who admits to having anxiety and explains why he cuts himself: "I feel nothing, I am nothing—I am empty." The pain is the only way he can feel alive.

## Prioritizing Our Children

Our children know how important they are to us when we clearly make them a priority in our lives. This means actually making them a priority in our schedules. For instance, choosing to stay at home with them instead of going out with our friends (a freedom which, once again, is made easier for French parents than American ones). Think about parents who put their children to bed as soon as they come home from work to have some peace and quiet, or who leave them with relatives or helping hands as often as possible to go away for weekends. These parents may very well show genuine care while attending to their children's basic needs. But in truth, these children feel unimportant to their parents, as the message hidden behind the adult behavior clearly indicates they are an impediment to how their parents really want to be spending their time.

Think about it: What would you think about a man who asked his friend or relative to give an engagement ring to his future bride rather than doing so himself? Wouldn't the young woman be justified in concluding that her fiancé obviously had better things to do than show his love for her? And wouldn't such an impression hurt her deeply and seriously undermine her self-confidence? In just the same way, when we put in only the bare minimum time for our children, even if we reassure them that they can always count on us whenever they are in need, it is always disastrous. Again: children invariably take such behavior as a sign of how little we value them.

Victor was a businessman who claimed he rarely had time to spend with his son, but never left his bedside when the boy suffered an acute peritonitis and was fighting for his life. When Victor realized that if, during an emergency like this, he was able to both work and fulfill his role as a father, he could and should also do so under normal circumstances. First, because the child was suffering from his father's constant absence, and second because he might otherwise conclude that, in the future, in order to get his father's time and attention, he needed to be on the verge death and consequently put himself in dangerous situations.

## Giving Our Children Clear and Regular Blocks of Time

The only sure way for our children to register our interest in them is to consistently demonstrate it by establishing regular blocks of time to be with them. It is indeed pointless for us to show an interest in them only on occasion, by taking them out to dinner or bringing them to a soccer match whenever it is convenient for us. Such sporadic activities do not suffice to convince our children they matter to us.

Indeed, children need reliable one-on-one time with us that they can count on no matter what—whether every evening, or in the case of divorced parents, every Wednesday or every other weekend—which should be something like twenty minutes at a minimum. Such blocks of time can go hand in hand with daily activities such as bathtime or dinner, as long as they don't entail off-putting chores like homework or tidying a room because it is important that, in those one-on-one moments with our children, we set aside our role as educator, and make it clear to them that our only agenda is to spend carefree and enjoyable moments with them. For instance, rather than inquiring about our children's grades at school or lecturing them about good manners, we should simply show interest in what they have to say, listening to their stories and asking them questions about their day. And we should do this whether our children answer or not, since they will eventually end up talking about themselves anyway, especially if we take care not to ruin these precious moments by grilling them or showering them with unsolicited nutritional or academic feedback. It's wiser to stick to topics that our children find interesting, such as their teachers or their friends. After all, we will have plenty of occasions to focus on discipline, preferably in real time, when they misbehave.

On the other hand, it's not a good thing to spend too much time with our children if it is for our own agenda, in order to feel or appear as good parents. In one case, "martyr parents" live their lives through their children, who in turn unfairly feel responsible for their parents' happiness or, worse, guilty of their unhappiness. Whereas "show-off parents" use their children as props with no consideration or respect for their taste or their needs, such as age-appropriate play or a healthy schedule. This accessorizing is literally the case, as we discussed, with celebrities who bring their children to fashion shows.

All of this is often fueled by the obsession with not doing enough for and with our children, which is increased by images spread on the Internet of "caring" parents who overdo their role either because of their anxiety or for the sake of appearances.

Moreover, any such performatively overt displays of caring behavior are harmful to children who will paradoxically feel neglected, and rightfully so, since such displays don't provide them with the proper nurturing (just as empty calories don't actually nourish you). Finally, they become confused and guilt-ridden since those feelings of neglect all seem so unfair toward their "caring, loving" parents. As a result, they bury these emotions in order to not feel this way.

## OVER-SUPERVISING OUR CHILDREN

This idea that more is better also seems to prevail when it comes to the supervision of our children. American parents are especially protective. The social pressure and disapproval are profound and—to European parents—incredible.

I have a young friend, Allie, who was recently out on bicycles with her three children, twin boys aged ten, and a girl aged six. They were all taking a single turn around her suburban block together, then planned to veer off toward the park. Allie was rounding the corner, last in line among the four of them, when she heard a woman who was still out of sight yell to the children: "Where is your mother?" This woman then said in an exasperated voice to her friend: "I cannot believe that their mother would let them out alone. Can you imagine the irresponsibility?" Allie then rounded the corner, coming into full view, and greeted these women with a stony silence. It's not the only such story I've heard, and we've all seen the newspaper articles detailing police calls for parents who have sent their children across the street to a park, or to take the city subway alone to school. As Leonore Skenazy, the founder of the Free-Range Kids movement, explains: "This very pessimistic, fearful way of looking at childhood isn't based in reality. It is something that we have been taught." Skenazy proceeds to argue that although parents' perceptions of danger have risen, childhood abductions and murders are at record lows.[10]

### Free-Range Versus Helicopter Parenting

The conflicts and tensions between groups of parents who believe children must be protected and accompanied at all times versus those who believe children must experience and practice failure on their own are increasing. Professionals are beginning to point to research indicating that helicopter-parenting attitudes lead children to be anxious and depressed and diminishes or even precludes resilience.

Consider the college student who saw a mouse in her dorm room and called the police, and other young adults who are similarly incapable of managing everyday life. According to the head of counseling at an American university where this issue was recently brought up in a formalized way, "Growth is achieved by striking the right balance between support and challenge. We need to reset the balance point. We have become a 'helicopter institution.'"[11]

In response to this growing awareness, "free-range" parenting may be on the rise, but not without powerful pushback that can even result in parents being arrested for so-called neglect. Free-range parents want their children to be independent, and to work up to independence with confidence gained by completing developmentally and age-appropriate tasks themselves. In the US, fear seems to drive the more mainstream parenting style whereby children are usually carefully ushered from one activity to another.

Free and self-directed play are taken out of the "schedule," and so are the confidence, the discovery of new skills and abilities, the experience of failure, and the development of resilience that are all part of such play.[12]

## How to Respect Their Need for Independence?

What is independence? It has nothing to do with creating a busy schedule for our children, which often amounts to "getting rid" of them, either because we want time for ourselves after work, or because, having failed to establish a deep and real relationship with our children, we have no idea what to do with them, or because we simply decide that we have better things to do.

It also has nothing to do with taking our children to dinner with friends, only to stick them down at the end of the table with the other similarly abandoned children, all of us telling ourselves there is no need to worry about them since they are with their peers. The truth is that prioritizing our own love life, or social and cultural activities, *at our children's expense*, amounts to telling them, "You're worthless." And the resulting low self-esteem, coupled with an intense feeling of guilt, will follow our children throughout their lives. By abandoning them in this way, we will have convinced them that they have done something wrong, or are inadequate or insufficient.

In fact, many of us parents indiscriminately invoke the concept of independence to ease our guilt when we are not taking care of our children. Let's face it, the goal of parenting is undoubtedly to prepare our children to be able to leave us when the time comes. That's what independence is. But the only real independence is the one children request, especially during adolescence. And even though this is a good thing, we often dread it because it inevitably plunges us into stress and anxiety, whereas the independence we expect young children to be capable of means nothing, and doesn't do them any good. It usually only serves the parents' interest to bring up the concept of independence early on in their children's lives as a way to avoid taking care of them instead of saying, "Do what you want and leave me alone," which would be far more honest.

More often than not, what such parents are after is not independence at all, but really a chance to abandon their children outright. It's absurd to think, for example, that young children ought to know how to play alone and occupy their time by themselves. Nine-month-old babies can neither walk nor play alone. They need someone to carry them and play with them. Likewise, when they reach childhood, even if it's possible to push them to be more independent, doing so means effectively imposing mental suffering, since they wouldn't yet have the emotional maturity to cope alone. It can certainly happen, but at what price? It's like pushing children to walk too early—they'll probably walk, but they may end up with bowed legs. Similarly, there is no virtue in sending small children to camp until their parents are sure that they can handle being away from their family, which is rarely the case before at least the age of six or seven.

It is better for us to wait for our children to be mature enough before suggesting certain activities from which they will only benefit once they are old enough to want to participate, and feel safe doing so. They will become independent when the time is right; when they are sufficiently secure in our love and the knowledge that we are there for them, they will have a chance to build themselves as individuals.

Imagine you need to pack a bag to go somewhere. If all your clothes are ready at hand, you will pack quickly and leave. Now imagine that I hid your shirts and socks. You are going to spend time looking for them. But since you cannot find them and because you know you will need them on your trip, you will end up not going. In fact, it's such a good way to force you to stay that if I didn't want you to leave me, I would hide all your clothes. It's exactly the same for children: if their parents do not give them enough love, they will stay home until they find what they are missing.

## The Importance of Helping Hands

Of course supervision is often totally necessary, as when we are working. It can also be a very good idea when—as is the case with all parents, from time to time—parents need breaks. A helping hand can be a family member, a babysitter, or a coach or a music teacher, during the span of a music lesson, a gym class, or longer. This support, whether occasional or regular, is all the more useful and justified in our contemporary society, which finds most of us living on our own rather than being surrounded by extended family, making it even more challenging for us to raise our children.

Considering how much our children are influenced and shaped by their surroundings and the smallest of experiences, however, it is essential that we parents be ruthless in selecting all the people who interact with them. We should assess the behavior and ideas of those helping hands to ensure that we would approve of everything our children might experience in their company.

We should be attentive to how our children react in the company of these helpers, while keeping in mind our children's best interests, not our own. This will minimize the risk of having them experience trauma that could've been avoided.

Such vigilance is one of the trademarks of good parents who are aware that they are the ones responsible if their children get bored, cold, unhappy, or even, God forbid, abused, when in the company of other caregivers, whether a music teacher, a priest, or a camp counselor. We should therefore avoid the slightest risk of putting our children through negative experiences, such as leaving them at a random daycare or with a new babysitter to go on vacation or out to a movie.

In short, it is wiser to stay with our children if the caretaker we have in mind doesn't inspire confidence or we dislike her in any way. And we shouldn't mind appearing difficult if we feel the slightest reservation or discomfort.

Asking for the support of helping hands has its upsides. Indeed, the caretaker, rather than being only a spare tire for us, is actually a plus for our children, allowing us to compensate for our lack of time, patience, taste, abilities, homework savvy, or skill at arts and crafts, sports, board games, or other activities.

Thus, contrary to popular belief, being a good parent doesn't entail making a point of playing ball with our children even though we hate sports, or of teaching them to ski despite our fear of heights. Rather, it implies being aware of our limitations and using a third party to help us when we rightly feel that our children should not be victims of our personal likes or dislikes. Good parents understand that their children deserve competent and positive mentors, as well as parents who truly enjoy what they experience with them and don't fake pleasure to be "kind" to their kids, because they can tell!

Additionally, working with third parties can be a very helpful educational tool. It can be educational for children, as extracurricular activities are a perfect base for discovering and affirming their likes and abilities, but also for parents, who get the opportunity to establish and enforce certain rules, such as the importance of persevering, once a commitment has been made, with chosen activities until the end of the school year.

As a result, there's nothing wrong with pushing our children to participate in a particular activity or asking them to stick to it, as long as we keep their best interest and capabilities in mind.

For example, it might be a good idea for parents to force an eight-year-old boy to continue skiing until the last day of winter break even if he wants to quit because he's upset he's not good at it, as doing so would lead him to work through his frustration and overcome a challenge. But it might be best they don't insist he go horseback riding if he's terrified of horses. By the same token, it might be just as wise to insist a little girl stay at overnight camp for the whole week even if she complains she is bored, so that she learns she is capable of surviving a week of boredom—especially if, in return, she's also promised that in the future she doesn't have to go back if she doesn't want to.

In short, it's a judgment call by the parents, who shouldn't hesitate to consult with the professionals taking care of their children—sports instructors, summer camp counselors—to help them determine what their children are really capable of doing. Indeed, one of the advantages of working with these outside helpers is that they are neutral and aren't as likely to project their unconscious desires and fears onto our children, as we might. They can help our children find their balance by allowing them to develop outside our gaze, which can be restricting even if well-intentioned. Outsiders can also be lifesavers to a child who is in the hands of a toxic parent, and needs to find normalcy and balance outside his own home.

## EDUCATIONAL AND EXTRACURRICULAR ACTIVITIES

It's no wonder that anxious parents end up doing too much with both educational and extracurricular activities. There is a cliché that arranging a variety of such options—karate, dance, language classes, tutoring, club soccer—is a sign of good parenting. But it's important that we parents not fool ourselves about what we are really up to when we give in to signing our children up for a trillion activities for so-called educational purposes. It can be an excuse for a number of issues we have as parents. We should ask ourselves very carefully whose interests we really have in mind.

Caring for our children doesn't mean overbooking them with violin lessons and Chinese lessons, back-to-back. Doing so can allow young, wealthy, and/or self-absorbed parents to justify avoiding spending time with their children. But it can also be an inadequate means by which to see ourselves as "good parents" or to hearten ourselves about our skills as parents. In any case the result is the same: we are neglecting our children and their desires.

Contrary to what we have always been told, it is far easier to use our power of suggestion to influence our children by shaping their aptitudes than to listen and respond to the needs they actually express.

Signing our children up for a trillion things is also very typical of those of us who want to reassure ourselves as educators. Some parents are so worried about doing a good job that they often engage in fierce competition with other parents, bragging about the number, variety, and originality of the activities they have their children signed up for. But the learning excuse, which reinforces this behavior, only benefits parents, fulfilling our own desires and soothing our insecurities, rather than giving our children the opportunity to explore their own desires and to develop their own identities at their own pace. Yet for children to develop, there is nothing quite like boredom, which forces them to build themselves as individuals, find their own path, and express their character. Therefore, it is essential that we give our children the space and time to do that, otherwise they are molded by our desires, not their own.

So how do we determine what is in our children's best interest rather than our own? For example, it's fair to want our children to learn how to swim at a young age so they don't drown, or have them take skiing, tennis, or piano lessons so they can participate in family activities. But it's disrespectful to try to turn them into "brainiacs," virtuosos, or accomplished athletes simply because it's important to us, makes us look good, or strokes our ego.

In fact, what really matters is our intention. Imposing activities on our children can stem from a concern for their well-being, as when we are convinced we have to do all we can to ensure their future in an increasingly competitive world. In this case, our notion of success drives us to raise the bar high. And even if it has other drawbacks, this approach is all the more legitimate because we are taking our children's best interest into account—a concept that varies considerably depending on our own culture, environment, and nationality.

Such was the case of Philippe, a French man who married Yong, a Korean woman. He disapproved of the pressure his wife put on their son to succeed at the national exam administered to all Korean eleven-year-olds, which determines whether or not the child will get to pursue a higher education. This proved a difficult situation since Philippe and Yong were, in their own way, both right: Philippe thought the pressure was crazy, and the exam itself didn't mean anything to him since it doesn't have an equivalent in France, while Yong wanted to secure her child's future in an Asian society where the competition is so intense that success is often limited to those students who get into the best universities.

## TAKING CARE OF OUR CHILDREN

As we've seen, there is, in fact, such a thing as taking "too much" care of our children, and helicopter parents are one of the examples of these excesses. But if we shouldn't overdo taking care of our children, what *should* we do?

### Being "Fully Present" When We Are with Our Children

What exactly would be the quality time we are supposed to spend with our children? At a minimum, we should expend the same amount of energy with our children as we would at a work meeting or playing tennis. We should make a concerted effort to remain attentive and focused, especially when we have a lot on our minds. First of all, if we allow ourselves to feel tired or distracted, we ultimately won't be able to enjoy the time spent with our children, just as we wouldn't enjoy a dinner with friends. Second of all, it is particularly crucial that we enjoy our time with our children for them to feel a sufficient level of interest from us in order that they can enjoy themselves, too, and be fulfilled and satisfied until we see them again.

Children can very well feel they have not seen us even when we were physically in their presence. For example, if we put them in front of the TV or a videogame to get some peace and quiet for ourselves; if we speak on the telephone without paying attention to them; if we talk to them in an absent and distracted manner; or if we run around doing several things at once, our children become as frustrated as if we had left them all by themselves. Feeling deprived, our children will then demand even more of our time and attention, which we will give only reluctantly since we feel like we have already done so. Eventually this creates a vicious cycle, whereby our children take on the role of the victim or bully, and we take on that of the tormentor or the bullied.

## Taking a Real Interest in Them

When parenting is all about parent performance, there is no room for the child. Does your interest in your child reflect back upon you, somehow, or does the interest make space for your child to emerge, bloom, and thrive as their own person? Of course we must pay attention to our children's progress in school, and keep an eye on their health, sleep, and diet, as well as their relationships with others. But we should also take an interest in the games they play, the friends they make, and the movies they like or dislike. And we have to read the book(s) they keep talking about, taste the juice they find delicious, or go to the restaurant they want to try. There is no other way to prove that we value them, that we care about their opinions, and, therefore, that they are important to us.

We must start showing our children our interest in them very early on rather than only once they share our own interests; the lasting bond we will have forged with them can in no way be created from scratch when they are thirty years old and we suddenly show interest in their love life or their work.

Taking a real interest in our children also means paying careful attention to what they say. The more interest we take in them, the more they express themselves freely, occasionally with no apparent rhyme or reason. For example, they might confide in us while coming out of the car or walking down the street, by expressing revealing statements like "So you've got problems with your sister too?" or by making out-of-the-blue requests that then need to be addressed and taken into account.

## Letting Our Children Do Their Part in Building the Relationship

All of this said, our relationship with our children should go both ways. In other words, we don't need to come up with the conversation or activity all the time, and we can and should let our children do their share of the relationship building too. Being truly attuned to our children and their unique needs often means we only need to respond to arising situations with flexibility and open minds. Very often, we should just sit back and remain on the lookout to respond appropriately to the needs that our children inevitably express, and which are often very different from those we anticipate. For example, if our child tells us he or she is sad and asks to be comforted, we might want to skip the activity we had organized for him or her prior to the conversation. We have to be ready for anything that comes up, just as we often are in our adult relationships. Imagine that your significant other comes back from work upset about something on an evening you had planned on going out dancing—wouldn't canceling those plans and staying home together be the best way to show you care? There's a strong chance that he or she would appreciate it much more than if you stuck to the original plan, no matter how romantic or well-intentioned. The same holds true with our children. They will be much more touched by the quality of our attention and the thoughtfulness of our responses to their needs than by our showering them with gifts or taking them to an amusement park.

Your child is a person. Every child has opinions, their own pace, their own tastes, their own everything. And they are supposed to let you know what they need. You have to give them space to do so. If you're filling up all the space, they have no space to be themselves. Being a good parent doesn't mean you're a great crafter or great inventor of imaginative activities and games. Let your children come up with ideas. They do have ideas and suggestions, and can be very creative.

# PART FOUR

# WAR

# AND

# PEACE

# 7

✐

# Structure and Discipline

*Childhood is a fragile stem that needs support.*

—SOSTHÈNE DE LA ROCHEFOUCAULD-DOUDEAUVILLE,
*The Book of Thoughts and Maxims*, 1861

I used to believe that children were delicate flowers. I had formed this idea from the fragmentary notions of psychoanalysis that had reached me, notions that emphasized the importance of childhood and its substantial effect on adult lives. I had also formed this belief on the basis of acute memories of my own childhood grievances, which incontestably endorsed how extremely sensitive children can be. I was therefore convinced I should treat my children like nitroglycerine, as if they might explode at the slightest shock. My heart ached with sadness and concern when they had the tiniest bump or cut, and their every wish felt to me like a sacred duty. Add to this my need to be loved and my absolute horror of confrontation, and I was the perfect cliché of an empathetic and permissive mother.

I believed that my infinite sensitivity in my dealings with my children could only be good for them, and the one thing that tormented me in my behavior was that I was incapable of self-control when I lost my temper or was frustrated by them. I strongly believed that this failing was the only thing tarnishing my behavior toward them, which was in all other ways positive and beneficial. I was all the more disheartened by this situation because it meant I yo-yoed between gentleness and anger, and I was conscious that this lack of coherence was bound to be harmful to my children.

Here again, I was entirely wrong. It would have helped me considerably if, at the time, someone had led me to understand that, much as my outbursts were a problem (although fortunately they derived from my past and not my own personality, so could be altered), my purported gentleness was equally problematic. It took me years to escape this infernal seesawing between authoritarianism and permissiveness, and to understand, define and eventually adopt a behavior that combined kindness with firm resolve.

## DEAD END NUMBER ONE: BEING TOO STRICT

At first, being a disciplinarian may appear to be an effective parenting method. This is because it allows us parents to directly shape our children's immediate behavior into what we want. It's also an easy approach for us to implement since we don't need to think or make the slightest effort to adapt our behavior to the circumstances, age, or character of our children. But beside these "upsides," this approach only has drawbacks. Jules Renard touches on this idea in his auto-biographical novel *Carrot Top*. The author describes his cruel and even sadistic mother's incessant bullying, which he deeply suffered from as a child. Begging only to be loved and unable to understand his mother's spite and contempt, the boy comes to wish that he were an orphan and decides to no longer love his mother. He demands to be sent to boarding school to escape this martyrdom. Only then, his mother breaks down crying, finally realizing the effect of her bullying on her son.

## A Counterproductive Method

The first downside to being a disciplinarian is that it is counterproductive; this method has more in common with training animals than educating humans, and leads to disastrous effects on children. Indeed, short term, if a child obeys his or her parents' orders, the array of violent and humiliating tactics involved in establishing this relationship based on fear and animosity will have the long-term effects of shaping the child in the image their parents project. Yet these parents ground their severity on the mistrust they have of their child: "He is going to try to fool me, lie, be lazy," and the negative presumption they have of him or her: "She is a liar, a crook, a loser." Thus, they likely push their child to become or do exactly what they fear most.

## A Method that Leads to Lies and Cover Ups

Another downside of being a disciplinarian is that it generates dishonesty among children who, wanting to avoid being punished by their parents, will inevitably re-sort to lying—sometimes to great lengths that defy all credibility.

Here's a little example that seems benign enough, but that repeated over time can lead to long-lasting behavioral patterns. When she was nine years old, Jenna was not allowed to eat ice cream. Too sweet, too expensive, too fattening, etc. She would nevertheless secretly buy ice cream with her cousin Daisy when they walked out around the neighborhood, and doing so was a joy to her. One day, at the ice cream stand, Jenna ran into Felicia, her grandmother's friend, and went into a state of panic. Daisy could see that Jenna was nervous and afraid—really terrified—and to her dismay, Jenna immediately cooked up the most incredible story, ribboned with lies and exaggerations, justifying why she was holding a cone in her hand just in case Felicia were to report the ice cream to Jenna's grandmother.

Even worse, being authoritarian fosters dissimulation. Children who fear talking to their parents will dare even less when it comes to serious matters such as bullying, racketeering, or sexual abuse. We should therefore worry rather than rejoice if our children appear perpetually happy and never cause trouble. The reality can only be one of two things: either they are protecting us because they see us as too weak to deal with their doubts and problems, or they are afraid of us, and don't want to risk talking to us about their true feelings. Healthy children always have questions to ask and opinions to share. And when they lie, it is only about little things, like when they answer "nothing" to the question "What did you do in school today?" only because they don't feel like discussing it.

## A Method that Deprives Children of Their Inner Compass

But that's not all. Being a disciplinarian with our children shifts their center of gravity, pushing them to behave according to the wishes of the adult wielding the carrot and stick. These children seek to please or oppose their parents instead of learning to trust their own judgment and feelings, which they need to rely on like a compass to navigate through their lives.

Teaching children to obey without question can prove quite dangerous. Just consider the damage produced by injunctions such as, "Listen to adults and do as you're told," that have made generations of children vulnerable to pedophiles and sadists because they had become accustomed to obedience. Or think of the harm caused by commands such as "Shut up," "Know your place," and "Who do you think you are?" All of these drive children to submit rather than react or respond.

Exposure to a disciplinarian cripples children, leading them to switch off feelings and sensations that they are forbidden to acknowledge, such as their own desire in any area of their lives, which they muzzle thoroughly as soon as we challenge it even in seemingly minor ways. Consider Adele, who couldn't understand why she never felt any desire and even panicked at the idea of ever wanting anything. This behavior lasted until, looking back, she remembered that her mother would give her the choice between a cookie or a waffle every day after school, and when Adele would reply, her mother would snap back, "Now you will get nothing. You take what you're given. You should never ask."

This restriction or lack of desire is likely to seriously damage a child's vitality by rendering them apathetic and even depressed for a long time; it is very difficult to revive one's desire once it has been repressed, even as an adult. The same can be said of fear and pain, which disciplinarian parents also want to tame by forbidding their children to complain. They often force their children to do what frightens them, and may even put them in danger under the pretext of "building character" or "toughening them up." Their argument? If one pays too much attention to children, they become "wimps" or "sissies." Yet precisely the opposite is the case. Children whose parents don't belittle or entirely discredit their discomfort get into the habit of paying attention to symptoms of this discomfort, and of taking care of themselves, all the more if their parents have instilled in them the feeling that they matter. Such assurance makes them more likely to avoid taking unnecessary risks. It also makes them more inclined to alert their parents as soon as they are in pain. Children conditioned in such a healthy way wind up avoiding many of the predicaments encountered by those who don't acknowledge what they feel, and who often end up acting irresponsibly and creating their own problems.

Such was the case of thirty-year-old Jaden, whose mother, a nurse, never took an interest in his health and repeatedly told him, "An Indian is never in pain." One day, while taking hang-gliding lessons, Jaden had a terrible accident from which he miraculously walked away with just a sore shoulder that he refused to acknowledge. He continued with the lessons until two days later, when his instructor pointed out to him that his shoulder had tripled in size and forced him to get it checked. It turned out he had broken his collarbone, scapula, and humerus.

Finally, disciplinarian parents stunt their children's sensitivity to emotions, which they then express unconsciously. This can cause children to develop psychosomatic symptoms or to place themselves in risky or dangerous situations. Take Harold, the protagonist of the 1971 film *Harold and Maude*, who wants nothing more than his mother's attention. While at boarding school, Harold provokes an explosion in chemistry class. He then returns home and hides. After listening to the police who've come to announce his death, his mother collapses. Harold then says, "I discovered that I really like being dead." He likes it because he has gotten a chance to measure the degree of sadness his mother felt at the news of his death.

Later in life, the young man simulates his death in a series of perverse scenarios to which his mother grows entirely indifferent. Faking his own demise becomes his favorite game until he meets seventy-nine-year-old Maude at a stranger's funeral. Whereas death is a very real prospect for Maude at her advancing age, it fascinates and delights Harold, who is still effectively a child. While he continues to stage his "suicides," Maude teaches him to love the whimsical life she leads and to break free from his morbid need for his mother's attention.

# DEAD END NUMBER TWO:
# BEING TOO PERMISSIVE

However, all the reasons that make being too strict a complete dead end do not make being too permissive a wiser path. This alternative is equally damaging for our children, as our society has clearly demonstrated, by switching from one extreme to the other, with parents going from "do as I say" to "do what you want."

## Betraying Our Children

At first, being permissive seems both kinder and less harmful to our children than being too strict, as it comes from our desire to be loved by them or from our fear of clashing with them. The sources of such lenient behavior strike many, at best, as understandable, and at worst, as forgivable acts of cowardice. Even so, being permissive falls under the category of abuse because it amounts to depriving our children of the emotional structure they need to feel reassured and to develop as well-adjusted individuals. This negligence, which would land any parent in jail if applied to their physiological needs, is fundamentally a betrayal of our children.

It is a betrayal because without set limits children are thrown into such a state of anxiety that they search desperately for these limits until they find some. Inevitably they act up, sliding little by little into delinquency or self-destruction. Failing to provide our children with the structure they need to become accomplished adults is itself an insidious form of harm.

Rose experienced her children's need for structure one day while vacationing with her two daughters, Piper and Melanie, ages three and five. The girls were cranky at the prospect of sightseeing, even though Rose had expressly tailored their activities according to their ages and interests. So Rose was very pleased to see Piper and Melanie cheer up when they started playing with the umbrellas she had bought earlier from a street vendor as a storm was looming. But when it started pouring, the elder daughter, Melanie, refused to stop playing and share the umbrella with her mother. At first, Rose hesitated to get angry because she didn't want to spoil her daughters' happy mood. But fortunately, she stuck to her sense of duty and raised her voice to insist Melanie share her umbrella. It was this lesson, along with all the others she would give her daughter throughout her upbringing, that would prevent Melanie from becoming a selfish and therefore insufferable adult.

This is why it is absolutely necessary to correct our children when they misbehave, whenever they are impolite, pretentious, disdainful, cruel, inconsiderate, or disrespectful toward others. We must set such limits for them, even if, as in the case of Melanie and Piper, their bad behavior initially seems trivial or insignificant because of their young age. To properly judge our children's behavior, we should imagine that same conduct on the part of an adolescent or an adult. If the behavior in question would strike us as unacceptable from an older person, then it is safe for us to conclude that we ought to discourage it in our children. And we must take immediate action. This was what happened with Melanie, who would have come off as an absolute brat had she behaved that way at the age of eighteen. The same holds true for young children who smack their peers or eat with their mouth open. Later in life, if they still don't know how to control their impulses, or if they still lack manners and respect toward others, they will be neither accepted nor appreciated by the people around them.

While it is fairly easy to scold five-year-old children, it is much harder when they are eighteen or twenty-eight years old, especially if they were never reprimanded for their misconduct when they were little. Therefore, if we can't bring ourselves to correct our children when they are very young, we are even less likely to do so when they get older. The sooner we set them straight, the better: it is unforgivable to let children get trapped and sink into bad behaviors that will only hurt them later on.

This clearly highlights how children, who appear to be coddled or spoiled, or whose parents acquiesce to them no matter the circumstances are in fact unloved, even abused. And we should think twice before assuming that extreme leniency toward our children is harmless. After all, permissiveness only makes sense if we consider our children incapable of improving their behavior and learning from what they are being taught, or if we simply don't care about their future.

## Whims and Wants

This view of permissiveness is not at all common or widespread; the first thing most of us think when the subject of leniency comes up is not our guilty negligence as parents, but giving in to our children's capricious behavior. But what if the root cause of such behavior came from the fact that we unfairly deem our children's genuine desires inappropriate, outrageous, or unjustified? Indeed, although children should not throw tantrums in order to get what they want, they probably wouldn't do so if we acknowledged their requests and responded to their desires as seriously as we do our own, instead of dismissing their wants as whims.

Take the classic example of a tantrum, where a child, whom we'll call Gavin, is screaming for sweets in a supermarket. Does the fact that Gavin wants something that inconveniences his parents mean that the boy's desire is a mere whim? Probably not, if we think about how we all have cravings, especially at the supermarket—places expressly designed to generate this type of impulse. Therefore, it would be unfair not to see Gavin's desire as legitimate. So perhaps the real problem is that Gavin screams in order to get what he wants. But then again, Gavin probably wouldn't scream if his parents took his craving as seriously as they would their own—for instance when they, too, feel like having something sweet—by considering Gavin's urge legitimate enough to acknowledge and respond to it, whether favorably or not.

Indeed, the fact that our children's desires are real and appropriate does not mean we always have to yield to them. It is our prerogative as parents to refuse. But we need to explain our decision to our children by saying, for example, "I don't want you to eat between meals," or, "I don't want to spend money," or even "I don't want you to eat sweets." These are all perfectly valid responses, whereas shutting our children down with statements like "You're just throwing a tantrum" is not. If we don't make the effort to explain our reasoning to our children, we hurt them just as surely as if we were to say: "No it's not true!" when they tell us they are in pain. In other words, there is no such thing as capricious behavior. And the necessity of recognizing our children's wants and needs as legitimate has nothing to do with caving in or being soft.

Olivia was bothered by the fact that her four-year-old daughter, Destiny, kept waking her up in the middle of the night because she was having nightmares. Olivia told her therapist, "It's just a trick; Destiny wants to sleep in my bed." Yet, during a recent session, Olivia had shared that a few days earlier she had woken up her husband and asked him to hold her in his arms because she had had a nightmare. Her therapist then responded, "In that case, your capricious behavior worries me more than your daughter's, because Destiny is only four and you're thirty-nine."

One day, Paul complained to his brother Charles about his children being ungrateful after he had taken them on a wonderful vacation in California. They showed no appreciation whatsoever. A little surprised by the response of his nephews whom he found adorable, Charles asked, "How long have they been asking for that trip?" To which Paul replied: "They never did, but it was amazing." Appropriately, Charles explained that ungratefulness meant not saying thanks for something that had been asked for, which was not the case with his nephews. Thus, they were neither spoiled nor ungrateful. The real question was, why did Paul feel the need to use his children and the belief that he was pleasing them as an alibi to please himself with this trip? So, the correct way for him to put it would have been to simply say: "We're going to California, whether you like it or not."

## Gifts

At the heart of clichés about leniency and permissiveness is the image of spoiled children showered with gifts. To spoil children is, in the true sense of the term, to damage them. And there are many ways to do so. We can damage them by burying them in gifts, since our apparent generosity, while satisfying our joy of gift-giving, stifles our children's desires and therefore deprives them of one of their drives in life. But we can paradoxically spoil and damage our children in the same way by not giving into them, whether out of harshness or principle. Indeed, if they are aware there is no chance their wishes will ever be fulfilled, our children will then do the only thing they know to avoid suffering: shut down their desires so as not to feel them anymore. In short, the quantity of gifts does matter. The more presents children receive, the less pleasure these presents bring them, since it's the scarcity of gifts that makes them invaluable.

But the *way* we give gifts also matters: it is definitely best for us to have a reason to give a present to our children. Indeed, when a present is equated with a reward, the efforts made to deserve it give our children the opportunity to overcome difficulties and succeed. The pleasure they get from the actual gift is enhanced by the satisfaction and pride they draw from their achievements.

That said, gifts are not of great importance in and of themselves, and this is true regardless of how much they cost, so long as they make sense within the family's economic circumstances. Our children need love, attention, and structure, not presents, even though gifts are nice to give and to receive. Presents are a problem if we give them to compensate for our lack of love, time, or structure. In those instances, gifts are symbolic of what's actually missing, and they become a stake between our children and us, as well as a symptom of the suffering caused by an unfulfilling relationship.

Such a manipulative use of presents often leads our children to throw tantrums and make demands that have less to do with the object itself—the gift requested—than with the void they feel. They develop an unfortunately life-long habit of projecting their feelings onto material objects, a habit that in turn can foster such behavioral problems as compulsive shopping, kleptomania, or shoplifting. If we give our children what they really need, the gift will remain just that—an object. Our children will enjoy having it, or regret not having it, but it will not encroach on what's essential; their emotional security will remain intact.

## ASSERTING AUTHORITY

Establishing that being a disciplinarian and being permissive are both dead ends doesn't help solve the problem for those of us who don't know what conclusion to draw from this, and often end up going back and forth between these two manners of behaving as parents. We need an alternative approach to authority—one that is based on our children's best interest.

## Establishing the No-nos

Our children's need for boundaries requires us to demonstrate some firmness, but only as long as it makes sense to
our children. Therefore, it is essential that we establish
clear, immutable no-nos that our children can comprehend
and respect. We also ought to be consistent and unwaver-
ing in how we enforce these non-negotiables so our children can both rely on these rules for structure and rebel
against them in order to build their individuality.

What are these no-nos? The best way to determine
them is by relying on what is in our children's best interest, in order to prevent them from harming themselves or
others—both physically and psychologically—so they can
become decent people appreciated by those around them.
We should teach them the rules of likability, which include
common decency, but also the moral values that are at the
core of such decency.

And we should enforce these no-nos when it comes to
all behaviors that could harm our children, short or long
term, even if these conducts fall into radically different cat-
egories, such as sticking their fingers in a socket, getting
themselves in trouble by not doing their homework, getting
high, or mistreating those around them, whether by talking
back or being rude or inconsiderate to us, their friends, or
a cashier.

It is crucial for us to enforce these no-nos by showing
our children a calm determination that leaves no room for
negotiation or opting out. And while it is important that
we explain these prohibitions to them, it is also crucial that
we accept appearing autocratic if our children are not old

or mature enough to understand, by saying, "I said no, because that's just how it is!"

## Calibrating Our Responses

### *Dealing with Our Children's Requests*

Contrary to popular belief, especially in France where there is a preconception that children are by essence spoiled brats, we should respond positively to our children's requests as often as possible. This shows them that they have good ideas and helps build their self-confidence, thereby preventing them from setting themselves up for failure down the road. Moreover, it shows our children that we respect their needs, validating their importance so that our children learn to pay adequate attention to them as well.

Besides, left to their own devices, children usually satisfy their needs quite naturally. They eat until they're no longer hungry and sleep however long they need— two obvious keys to good health. In addition, the more we respond favorably to our children, the more their requests become objectively reasonable and legitimate. Children who have grown accustomed to being heard and taken seriously will clearly articulate their needs, by saying, for example: "I need a hug" instead of smashing a plate and forcing us to decipher what we see as a tantrum.

In numerical terms, we should respond positively to, say, 75 percent of our children's requests until they reach the age of ten—at which time they can start to do certain things on their own without our permission. Furthermore, we should respond positively to our children even if they are shy about formulating those requests, or if their demands seem relatively inconsequential. This approach only has upsides; when our children understand they have an influence over our schedules and time management—for example, when we cancel an evening out if they ask us to stay with them or if they tell us they are sad to see us go—they soon learn to choose their requests carefully.

Such was the case with Kimberly, a young woman working from home who would send her thirteen-year-old son Kenneth to the pediatrician, a neighbor in their same building, on his own. The day Kenneth requested her company on one of these trips to the doctor, Kimberly complied at the expense of canceling an appointment with a client, thus demonstrating to her son that she was taking his request seriously. But at the same time, she took the opportunity to explain that her work wouldn't always allow this much flexibility, and would sometimes prevent her from joining him on future trips to the doctor or elsewhere. And when we don't respond positively, we should still address and acknowledge our children's requests.

Not too long ago, I was in a shoe store in the US. I overhead a man hollering above the conversations of many people in the crowded store: "What? What? No! No!" I turned to see a man twisting up his face in disgust at his son, who must have been about ten or eleven years old. The man then turned to his wife and explained, maintaining his disgusted expression: "He says he wants the shoes that light up with the remote control. I said no! No!"

I watched as the boy, all eyes upon him, walked quietly away from his father. Imagine if instead his father had said in a steadier voice: "Oh, the shoes that light up with a remote control! What an amazing idea. They're fun to look at, aren't they? I might have wanted those too, as a boy. But I'm afraid they are too expensive, and they don't seem very practical..."

Our authority is that much greater when we limit the no-nos we establish. Therefore, as essential as it is for us to be uncompromising when we enforce our rules, it is as important that we grant as many of our children's requests as possible. Because our children, who function according to imitation and reciprocity, will show us the same benevolence and attentiveness we have showed them.

However, responding favorably to our children's requests doesn't mean responding to them immediately. In fact, sometimes we should wait a bit before granting our children's wishes: rushing to fulfill our children's demands as if they were emergencies suggests they are in some kind of danger, and this fosters a feeling of anxiety in our children as well as in us. On the other hand, frustration—in small doses—has educational value; it acclimates our children to the idea that they might not always get what they want, or at least not right away, and that they are perfectly capable of handling it.

But there is no need to orchestrate this frustration, since we need only put our baby down for a brief moment in order to light the stove or run a bath, or be slightly late when picking up our children from school, for them to realize that their wishes are not met all the time. We should

therefore learn to dose this frustration, which is only beneficial to our children if it is limited to, say, 20 percent of
what they experience, and if it results in a positive outcome. Our children will learn to handle their frustration
once they no longer associate waiting with displeasure,
whereas they won't be able to if waiting too often results in
suffering and disappointment.

### Scolding

It is essential for us to scold our children as soon as their
behavior becomes a problem and we want to see it end.
For example, a two-year-old who goofs around every night
needs to be told that enough is enough. And even though
we may fear we'll traumatize our children or we believe we
shouldn't scold them since we are supposed to respect their
feelings, we should not give up our authority; firmness is
essential for our children's emotional safety. Indeed, letting
our children run the show sends them the signal that we
aren't stronger than they are, and that we are therefore incapable of guiding and protecting them, which provokes
huge anxiety.

This firmness is indispensable, regardless of the explanations I gave earlier about children's sleeping disorders
often being a response to their parents' unconscious desires. Whether or not we understand the real reason for
our children's sleeping problems, and whether or not these
problems are in response to us, it is out of the question to
let our children have it their way because it is harmful for
them not to get the proper amount of sleep. Therefore, we
should put them back to bed, firmly saying, "No, you need

to go to sleep," so that they are able to get into a healthy sleep pattern.

In short, we should not hesitate to reprimand our children, even fifteen-month-old babies, if they, for example, raise a hand to us or bang their head against a wall, by saying: "I'm not interested in your shenanigans. You need to stop right now." Because it works. Indeed, our children are so pragmatic, they stop any behavior from which they don't benefit. Conversely, if we show concern instead of reprimand, our children will pick up on this right away, and, thrilled to discover their power to manipulate us, they'll want to use it again by opposing us at the next opportunity.

### Knowing When to Back Down or to Do Nothing

We shouldn't overdo the reprimanding, however. It is indeed important for us to evaluate our children's inadequate behavior in relation to their own good, and learn to put it into perspective if it doesn't undermine their best interest. For example, a mother is probably right to give in to her baby boy who refuses to fall asleep in his crib if he's not rocked for ten minutes, because it's no big deal. This is especially the case if the child's behavior doesn't conform to a pattern, or his typical way of being—if the child, for instance, demands more from his mother than his grandmother, or vice versa. Indeed this means that his behavior, which may cause problems of fatigue or organization to those around him, is hardly representative of his personality.

But sometimes, the best way for us parents to react is to ignore our children's behavior. This was the case with Mason, the four-year-old son of Riley, a nutritionist. Mason found that his mother did not take an interest in him and, to get her attention, declared, "I'm not hungry." But since this brought no reaction from Riley, Mason then said, "So you don't care?" "That's right," Riley replied. "If you're not hungry, you don't eat—it's that simple." To which Mason then replied, "Yeah, well then, I'm hungry."

### Punishing

However, we sometimes need to resort to sanctions, which should ideally be proportional to our children's offense.

This point is illustrated in a brilliant scene featured in a Canadian sitcom, in which a woman asks her teenage son to clean his room. He replies, "Why bother? There's no point to it, since I'm just going to mess it up again in three hours!" Cut to the next scene, in which the same teenager asks his mother when she is going to make dinner, to which she responds, "Why bother? There's no point to it, since you're just going to be hungry again in three hours!" After that, we see the rattled teenager utter, "Okay fine, I'll clean my room, but then, you make me something to eat!"

Indeed, in this case, the mother's response focuses on what's essential for her child, namely to show him the impact of his words. And that is precisely what sanctions are for: making our children realize the consequences of their actions when it is preferable for them not to experience those consequences directly.

Take, for example, Betty, a young child who commits a petty theft. There is no doubt that it is preferable for her parents to sanction her, either by forcing Betty to return the stolen object, writing a letter of apology to the owner, or by forbidding her to play video games for a month, rather than have Betty face the full legal consequences of her act, beginning with a trip to the police station.

Indeed, resorting to punishments is only advantageous if we keep in mind our children's best interest. We should do everything we can to avoid humiliating or dominating our children when we conceive and apply these sanctions. This wouldn't have been the case for Betty's parents in the previous example had they resorted to corporal punishment, or banned her from playing video games for a year. Such a humiliating or disproportionate response would translate more into a desire to dominate rather than educate their child.

Of course, if we lash out when we are infuriated and unintentionally slap or spank our children, it has nothing to do with our desire to dominate. In such cases, our reaction mainly reveals that we feel powerless, because we don't know how to verbalize our emotions, especially anger, and so we compensate for our inadequacy. What matters then is that we first apologize, and next, reflect on our behavior. In order to keep from responding this way again, we need to clearly identify our behavior as a slip-up rather than resorting to some educational alibi to try to justify ourselves.

## PICKING OUR BATTLES

What is parents' authority but what our children bestow on us, whether it is skill, wisdom, knowledge, or experience? This fact ought to lead us to use our authority sparingly, like a precious commodity, by limiting ourselves as early as possible to being a role model and source of advice during ongoing exchanges with our children. In return, they will then limit their oppositions to us to the minimum they need in order to develop as individuals. Conversely, an overly strict upbringing, as we have seen, will most likely lead our children to feel terrible, and antagonize us in dangerous ways as a result.

So, to remain effective and influential, we ought to carefully pick our battles and simply settle for enforcing the few rules we deem essential. We shouldn't squander our authority on minor matters such as bedtime, food, or fights between siblings, as many parents do. Because, if we keep nagging or screaming at our children to have them clean their room or eat vegetables, our authority will be so blunted that they won't listen to our input on important issues or during a true crisis.

This is exactly what happened to Lauren, who, convinced she was doing the right thing for her daughter Trinity by using her authority on all fronts, chose to focus on and criticize Trinity's obsession with designer clothes, rather than celebrating her academic and social successes. Fortunately, Lauren soon realized that this was rather ridiculous, or else possibly rooted in a need to dominate, which didn't reflect well on her and was obviously not in Trinity's best interest.

Moreover, the authoritarian measures we take on such minor issues are almost always counterproductive and ultimately have a boomerang effect in that the frustration they induce in our children often backfires. Indeed, no one can keep from thinking about and wanting what he or she is denied. Take the right to vote, for example. We don't ever think about this because it is a given right, but if it were abolished, its absence would prove unbearable and immediately turn into an obsession. In the same way, prohibiting sweets, forcing our children to eat vegetables, or imposing a strict bedtime will only result in making sweets irresistible, vegetables detestable, and bedtime a constant source of discord, upset, and anxiety.

Similarly, rules designed to establish quotas for how many sweets are okay or how much video gaming time is allowed completely monopolize our children's attention and energy. They can then only focus on respecting, bypassing, or violating these rules. Therefore, these rules only end up dominating the exchanges between our children and us, preventing any substantial discussion or debate about the real underlying issues at stake. Additionally, they prevent our children from feeling and realizing the drawbacks of their excessive behavior on their own—namely, experiencing nausea or disgust from eating too many sweets, or the isolation that comes from playing video games for exorbitant amounts of time, not to mention the tangled feelings inherent in living in a fantasy world where actions like killing have no consequences. Therefore, we need to implement these quotas sparingly. And before we do, we should try suggesting attractive and rewarding alternatives by offering to bake a cake with our children, play a board game, or go outside for a game of softball, because the fun they will have during these interactions with us will hopefully lure them away from their iPad or the TV screen much more judiciously and permanently than discipline alone.

## Meal Time

So many of us parents have rules regarding food and eating, all of which ultimately lead to regrettable tensions between our children and us. This is especially ill-advised since nutritionists everywhere now agree that anyone bombarded with dietary information or advice comes to abandon his or her inner sensations of hunger and satiety, and risks developing food anxiety or, worse still, an eating disorder. Chances are that children who are forced to eat vegetables will develop a dislike for them, just as children prohibited from eating sweets will hide to eat candies or obsess over them. As for the children who are put on a strict diet, they are doomed to crack and down a whole pack of cookies, or tons of chocolate, whereas they otherwise would have been more likely to be satisfied with just one piece.

The wisest response for us when it comes to our children's eating habits is therefore to be patient with them and to make food and meal time a pleasure instead of an ongoing challenge. Such efforts entail that we share with them warm, convivial, well-balanced, and if possible, tasty meals, without commenting on the food's dietary content and benefits, nor forcing them to eat if they are not hungry or refuse to, but without offering to fix them something else if that is the case. In all likelihood, our children, who are naturally curious, will eventually come to appreciate what is repeatedly offered to them, like fresh fruits and vegetables—all the more if they see us enjoying those foods ourselves.

The same can be said for enforcing good manners. Incessantly repeating "Sit up straight" or "Close your mouth when you chew" is useless. Indeed, it's better to settle for the occasional, friendly reminder like, "And there, your elbows, are they in the right place?" and above all to set a good example by putting these precepts into action in front of our children because—as is often the case—leading by example is incredibly effective. This easygoing approach when it comes to good manners is all the more sensible if we keep in mind that our children may very well have assimilated these rules so as to follow them perfectly when at their grandparents' or a friend's house, but don't apply them at home where they need to recharge and relax.

## Bedtime

Bedtime also gives rise to conflicts and power struggles, turning it into another challenge layered with stress and tension when it should be a gentle and peaceful time. The pity is that without our involvement, our children fall asleep when they are tired, and if they haven't slept enough on a given night, they quickly understand that they need to go to bed earlier the following evening.

So why do we get involved? We often want to put our children to bed to get some peace and quiet after a long day, understandably. But instead of openly admitting that's the real reason, we tell our children it's for their own good. Inevitably, they perceive and interpret it as punishment and they are probably right, since, as we have seen, we often reproduce our own parents' behavior, whether to avenge or validate it, by inflicting the same distress we experienced on our children. In other words, we likely impose the same bedtime on our children that we ourselves were subject to, and generally, we just need to realize this in order to stop making bedtime an issue.

Our children are perfectly capable of understanding that we don't want to take care of them around the clock. They will easily accept going to bed, provided they feel they have spent enough quality time with us that day, and they are allowed to hang out in their room by themselves until they are ready to go to sleep. This is even more likely to be the case if we have been up front with our children and explained that we need a break (which is still an excuse we should not overuse, otherwise it would indirectly amount to denying our children their existence) rather than relying on the classic argument "It's for your own good." We only need to say: "Go play in your room and do what you want until you fall asleep because I need some peace and quiet." An honest approach is educational and all the more welcome; when the time comes, it will allow our children to have the same self-caring response toward us without any feeling of guilt when, for instance, they leave us behind to go party with friends, or move out into their own place once they are old enough.

## Chores

Household chores, another sticking point between our children and us, happen to be all the more unnecessary when we consider the unscheduled time children need in order to develop at their own pace. This includes experiencing boredom—a condition that is increasingly rare in our children's lives today between school, homework, extracurricular activities, and multiple screens filling up every hour of every day. Besides, is asking our children to participate in household chores really a key to a successful upbringing? The best way to make them understand they must take care of their things is to let them experience the consequences of not doing so as soon as they are old enough—roughly around the age of eight. Let them notice how difficult it is to find their toys after not having put them back in their place, or experience that the pens they didn't recap no longer work, for example. They will see! And this should encourage us to either stop cleaning our children's room, or continue to do so if we can't stand their mess, but certainly not force our children to pick up after themselves out of some educational principle.

As for the apparent symbolic value of these chores, it remains to be proven. It is pointless and even counterproductive to ask our children to help us at a young age with the expectation that they will become helpful and obliging adults as a result. Indeed, they will only be considerate of others if we were considerate of them. That is, if we respected their needs as children by sparing them adult tasks in favor of allowing them to develop peacefully and at their own pace, which is often labeled as selfish. This also means being up front when asking them for their help and calling it a favor (something they will very likely do gladly) instead of attempting to manipulate them with various claims about their own good, work ethic, and so forth.

## Siblings

Finally, the last topic on which we often squander our authority: siblings. Our duty is to keep our children close to each other by being careful not to create jealousy, which is neither automatic nor inevitable. This effort begins with the birth of the younger child. We have to make our elder child feel that the arrival of the newborn brother or sister is not going to change our love for him or her, nor the attention he or she receives. In order to do so, we should start by refraining from saying things like, "I can't take care of you the way I used to" or "You need to make room for the baby." But also, contrary to popular belief, during the first few months of our youngest child's life, we ought to favor the older child when he or she demands something at the same time as the baby.

Imagine Ingrid, a newborn baby girl. She can wait a few minutes for her bottle or a diaper change. But Sam, her older brother, needs his parents to immediately reassure him through concrete and clear proof that his place in their hearts and home is not at risk. From then on, if his parents understand this, Sam's anxiety has no reason to persist, because if he is confident about his importance in the family, he will spontaneously encourage his parents to take care of Ingrid when she cries, just as he would tell them to turn off the stove if he noticed the milk boiling over—in both cases Sam would understand the need and consider his parents' response to Ingrid normal, even preferable.

Additionally, we should get involved as little as possible in our children's relationships with each other. Best, for example, to simply validate the spontaneous reactions of our older child toward a newborn with statements like, "How great, you're really behaving like a big brother/big sister" rather than assigning him or her the role of the one who is in charge of protecting his or her sibling, or setting a good example. We also need to avoid asking our older child to take care of the youngest; the role of the eldest isn't that of a babysitter, and he or she shouldn't be treated as free help. An older sibling is also not emotionally or intellectually equipped for this task, which therefore has no educational value for him or her.

Finally, we should not mediate our children's fights with each other, or at least as little as possible—perhaps only 30 percent of the time, when it appears the siblings can't resolve some issue between themselves. Indeed, more often than not, when we intervene, we blur our children's feelings and understanding of the situation. We wind up depriving them of the inner compass they need to control their aggression and how often they fight, and therefore their ability to quarrel without harming each other, like puppies do when they play rough. By intervening we're likely to cause trouble where there really is none.

We should also avoid intervening because we often don't understand the subtleties of the situation we're entering into in our attempts to end disputes between or among our children. We may very well accuse the wrong child and punish the eldest when in reality the youngest is the one who caused trouble, for instance; this then discredits our authority and fosters resentment among siblings.

If we do choose to intervene, however, the best solution for us is not to mediate, but to find some way for our children to reconcile at our expense. We could for example say, "You don't have to get along, but you do have to stop bugging me. So, you'll each stay in your room and stop speaking to each other." Because chances are our kids, bummed to be isolated, will try to defy our sanction by finding secret ways to communicate with each other, and in the end forget why they were fighting in the first place.

Put another way, we should be wary of our inner capacity to provoke jealousy between our children without realizing it. Take Martha, a mother of three, who invited her friend Naomi over for lunch, and asked her two older daughters to be quiet so they wouldn't wake up their six-week-old sister who was sleeping in the room next door, while asking her friend if she would like some salad in the same breath. This shocked Naomi, who then gave Martha the sign to be quiet and gestured toward the whiteboard that was hanging on the wall, before explaining that if the girls had to keep quiet to avoid waking the baby, then really everyone needed to be quiet, including the grown-ups. Otherwise, Martha's method was only going to make her older daughters resent their baby sister.

It is especially important not to provoke our children's jealousy since this bond between siblings gives them a special space where they can mutually complain, comfort, and protect each other from us parents, making them stronger and better prepared to deal with the challenges of life in turn. That may very well be why we often see a difference between first children, who are more tense and nervous than their younger siblings, who feel secure and protected by the older ones.

## Adolescence

Adolescence is a tense and tricky time between our children and us. They need to oppose us, and we shouldn't shield ourselves from this confrontation as long as it doesn't develop into a conflict. Indeed, it is important that we remain strong and firm in our positions, so as to be pillars of stability in our children's eyes while they go through significant physical and psychological changes.

We can start by dialing down our anxiety about our children's future. After all, it is up to them to find their way, and not for us to dictate their conduct, nor suggest which education or job they should choose, because that would ultimately mean that we are the ones deciding for them. Also, there is a good chance they have already picked up the fundamental values we have been teaching them all along. It's unlikely that they will become white supremacists if we are liberal intellectuals, for example, unless they want to punish us for something or if we were too tough while they were growing up. We should relax and strike a balance between what we would like our children to become and what we will allow them the space to become.

Here again, we must choose our battles. Unlike the earlier years, though, when we needed to stand firm on the essentials and lighten up on the smaller stuff, we should now do the contrary: oppose our teenage children on harmless subjects, for instance by questioning their wardrobe or challenging their political opinions, in order to avoid picking fights on important topics, such as schoolwork, which might lead them to sabotage their grades. We should not hesitate to overplay our opposition on innocuous topics.

For example, if we are annoyed by our teenager's taste in music, we better express it loud and clear by saying, "Turn down that hideous noise!" or "I hate your music."

But don't we usually do the exact opposite of this? We hound our children about important issues such as drugs or schoolwork, and try to play buddy-buddy with them about their music taste, for example, hoping that it will ease the tension. Maybe, we think, if we allow them to get a tattoo or pretend to like their music, we'll appear to be cool parents and win them over a little more. But our children don't want this complicity; they prefer that we act our age and of our generation. If indeed we act our age and of our generation, we won't feel the need to spend all of our time with teenagers like them, which would in turn give them the space to not feel guilty about not wanting to be with us anyway (and at this age, they *shouldn't* want to be with us all the time!). We should resist the temptation to play young and cool or buddy-buddy, which only pushes our teenage children to want to distinguish themselves from our generation by doing more extreme things than we do, for example, by taking hard drugs if we smoke pot (in our attempt to display coolness).

❯❮

# 8

# Bonding with Our Children

*Children need models more than critics.*

—JOSEPH JOUBERT,
*On Education (III)*, 1866

One of my children once wanted to hug a homeless person on the corner of our street, hoping to embody the precepts of generosity and care for other people that I tried instilling in them. I must confess that my first thoughts were concerns of hygiene rather than charity, but I ultimately realized we could do more good by bringing a meal for the old man instead. This incident was a wake-up call for me, because I grasped that the lessons in ethics and morals that I was giving my children had to take into account real life situations, notably the dangers of approaching strangers, but above all my own mixed feelings and contradictions. Indeed I could not hope my children would adhere to the principles I was teaching them if I failed to tell them the truth. The result of this realization was that I tried to stop pretending to be a better person than I was, and instead started answering their questions as frankly as I could (while of course being careful to make my replies age-appropriate). All of this meant I began explaining the world to them as it was rather than as it should have been. In other words, I began to teach them how complex life really can be. And this is one of the things that makes me most proud, since the resulting rich and honest intellectual exchange forged between us a genuine and strong connection while improving my children's ability to assimilate new information and real life situations.

The reason this transformation in me was so important is that it eliminated phoniness from my teaching. Even good ideas, in order to come through and be accepted, need to be brought down to earth and adapted to each parent's true personality. This resulting genuine connecting was everything, since what I began to realize is that the key to raising our children successfully lies in the quality of the bond we create with them.

This bond requires that we respect our children. And there again, I had many preconceived ideas about the way I was supposed to behave with them, which went against my natural inclinations and true self. I am a naturally empathetic person and a very good listener, almost always doing my best to understand the needs of my friends and partner. But I was convinced that I had to act differently as a mother. Indeed, I thought I would be surrendering all of my parental authority if I was too nice and too often considered my children's demands appropriate or acceptable. I've come to learn this is a very widespread notion—many people think that it is a parent's duty to label their children's requests as whims and to rebuff them, often resulting in treating their children worse than their next-door neighbors without even realizing they're doing so.

What I discovered was that the respectful way to behave with my children was to show them the same consideration I extended to others, without of course treating them as if they were adults. But this approach requires all the more effort and reasoning if we ourselves were not respected as children. Indeed, in that case, this respectfulness can strike us as absurd and even inappropriate, or we might have a hard time understanding and assimilating what kind of exchange it entails, and what kind of bond we should aim for.

## COMMUNICATING

For starters, we have to establish constant communication with our children. Happy, healthy children are always asking questions about what their parents are experiencing—relentless indeed! We've probably all felt a little irritation with these never-ending questions. But we must answer these questions truthfully no matter the topic, even those that may not seem child-appropriate or to be any of their business. Apart from our own sex lives, which really must remain taboo, there is no subject off-limits to children. And we should be able to talk about everything with our children, provided we tailor our comments to their age and comprehensive abilities. Therefore, it's mostly up to them to determine what is their business and what is not. Indeed, children seek only to validate what they perceive in our adult world before moving on to something else, usually a topic that concerns them directly and captivates them more. This is exactly what they do when our response co-incides with what they feel.

For example, a young girl might sense that her parents have quarreled and are momentarily on non-speaking terms, but she can only speculate since she can't be sure of it—her parents are putting on an act of friendliness in order to keep her out of their argument. Chances are, if she feels free doing so, she will ask them questions to validate what she is sensing—that they have indeed been arguing. (All the worse if for one reason or another she does not feel free to ask such questions.) It would be better for her parents to simply be up front and tell her in the first place that they are in disagreement about something, making them tense, but that it is only for a while. The girl would thereby understand she has nothing to do with the issue, subsequently lose interest in the matter, and go back to minding her own business and being a kid.

Aside from their questions, another integral part of our communication with our children involves their requests, and we should devote a large part of our dialogue to these requests. All the more because positive or affirmative responses can lead to all sorts of lessons, including surprisingly unconventional ones. Take the previous example of Gavin, who asked his parents for chocolate at the supermarket: by agreeing to get him some, and even to let him eat astronomical amounts of it, they allowed Gavin to experience the nauseating effect of having eaten too much chocolate, and to therefore learn the virtues of moderation.

The response of Gavin's parents is very different from that of overly lenient parents who give in out of weakness or lassitude. But a response like this one requires that we think ahead about our positions and priorities as parents—based only on our children's best interest—so that we can treat their demands with coherent responses. Let's face it: we can't afford to give in to our children's demands the first three times out of weakness only to refuse them on the fourth for no reason. Our children have a keen sense of logic and fairness, and they will immediately detect the flaw in our reasoning.

But this doesn't mean we have to be infallible! It would be oppressive and awful for children to have perfect parents (whatever that may be) and there are valuable lessons in honesty to be learned when we make mistakes and acknowledge them by "going back" on our words or actions. If we instead fail to let go of our mistakes and errors, by rigidly clinging to our initial (albeit mistaken) point of view, our children will be frightened by our lack of judgment or insight and won't trust us enough to confidently comply and follow our lead.

This was the case for Joseph, age sixteen. His parents were so eager to see him pick science as his primary course of study in high school that they claimed he would not be able to study economics in the future without having first taken science courses. This was probably true in their own day but was no longer the case. Their unfounded argument discredited them in Joseph's eyes—a serious shift in the eyes of an adolescent who is beginning to distance himself from his parents in a developmentally appropriate way. Fortunately, his parents eventually had the good sense to verify their claim, discover they were wrong, and recognize their mistake. As a result, their connection with Joseph was strengthened beyond even where it had been prior to their having made a false claim.

When a situation surprises us, we also have the right to not know what to do, say, or how to react. But, again, we should communicate this to our children.

Consider Nathan, a nineteen-year-old French undergrad, who went to his parents to ask for their advice after having been verbally attacked by one of his professors, who told him he was "as dirty as a pig." Although Nathan's parents were appalled by the teacher's violent insults, initially they didn't know how to advise their son. They reached out to their friends for advice, some of whom were familiar with the teaching methods in Jesuit Colleges, and learned that professors would often be aggressive with their top students, once they spotted them, with the intent of "toughening them up" so that these students would be better prepared to handle the pressure of finals. Nathan's parents subsequently shared this with their son and told him the choice was nevertheless his: refuse to put up with his professor's way of teaching and change schools, or ignore the verbal abuse that was evidently nothing personal and stay at the school to benefit from its excellent academics.

Critically, however, the communication with our children cannot be a one-way street. Just as parents bring up questions and conversations, children ought to be allowed to do the same, since this will teach children how to think and sharpen their arguments. But it requires that we be absolutely loyal to our children and treat them as valid interlocutors rather than agreeing with them just to make them happy, or to avoid conflict. It also means we should be willing to agree with our children's point of view when their argument is simply better than ours, or be ready to teach them what they don't yet know in order to help them develop and enrich their reasoning.

Take Genevieve, who forbade her son Ethan, nine, to walk to school on his own—an order Ethan challenged, since he found it contradictory. His mother was constantly telling him how much she trusted him, but then behaved in a way that seemed to say she didn't. Genevieve admitted that she was baffled by Ethan's argument and asked for some time to think before responding—which Ethan rightfully interpreted as a tribute to his intelligence. In the end, Ethan willingly complied when his mother came back with the argument about the limited peripheral vision of a nine-year-old, which could put him at risk—this allowed Genevieve to both maintain her ruling and her trust in Ethan.

The example is interesting because it demonstrates that a respectful exchange of views between parents and children can lead to a confrontation, even a conflict, which we shouldn't be afraid of. It is indeed beneficial to our children because it forces us to fulfill our role as parents while helping them build confidence in their own judgment, which will eventually lead them to feel comfortable offering advice to others, such as their own friends or coworkers. But with this type of respectful exchange, we also gain credibility and authority in our children's eyes, who in the end won't suspect us of just wanting to be proved right when we make our arguments.

Such was the case with Aaron, a teenager who wanted to try bungee jumping but was forbidden to do so by his mother, who was too frightened by the idea. He ended up renouncing his plan because he recognized that his mother had often made an effort to get over the anxiety she had about him doing things. Aaron realized that her fear about him bungee jumping was deep and genuine, and since he didn't want to cause her distress, he abandoned the idea.

Though sometimes difficult and often burdensome, this type of communication is the key to solid and long-lasting relations of mutual trust and respect with our children.

## TRANSMITTING

Our role as parents doesn't end with open communication in and of itself, as we also have a duty to take full advantage of this communication to transmit all our knowledge and thoughts to our children.

### Values

This transmission starts with our values, the main one being—in most cultures and religions—caring for others. It is a humanistic value essential to us as social beings in a society that, now more than ever, needs empathetic people who reach out to and connect with others. We also have a duty to transform the society of tomorrow by transmitting the values of work, effort, and civic duty—to name just a few important virtues—that any reasonable person would agree are sorely needed in today's difficult world.

As with learning a foreign language, our children must internalize values gradually, through a learning process that requires a lot of repetition and many explanations. We shouldn't expect our values to be transmitted through abstract sermons and lectures; the only way to get our point across to our children is to teach them little by little throughout their lives, and by example.

What a great opportunity, then, to make use of ordinary circumstances as they come up to explain, comment, and illustrate our positions to our children. For example, to get them to understand the important principle of keeping their word, we can forbid them from canceling an invitation that they had previously accepted, even or especially if something better comes up that they would rather partake in.

The most important thing—the one thing you must not waver on—is your values. At the end of the day, bedtime doesn't matter, the daily schedule doesn't matter, the perfect meal and snack plan don't matter. The kindness and golden rule—if those are your values—are what matter. Imagine you are rushing home to get your child their healthy meal on time, in order to be in bed on time, and while at the grocery store, your son is harsh and rude to the cashier. This is a perfect example of enforcing a value and not letting go by thinking: he's tired, he's hungry, we're in a hurry. Whatever the values most important to us— perseverance, work, empathy, honor, integrity—we must defend them on a daily basis in concrete ways, and forbid our children from engaging in behavior that contradicts them by correcting their mistakes in real time, and by encouraging them when they do the right thing.

Of course, none of this works if we don't respect these values ourselves. Just as the best way to learn a foreign language is to try to mimic those who speak it, the best way for our children to appropriate moral values is to imitate those who exhibit them, beginning with us, whom they imitate in all things anyway. Our children must see for themselves that we don't content ourselves with just giving praise to generosity, for example, but that we actually do reach out to others, whether it is at the park, the supermarket, or in the subway, and that we truly care, even when we are faced with people who are different from us, in appearance, background, or political or religious beliefs. We need to demonstrate examples of giving so that our children can assimilate what it means to be generous, little by little.

When we profess our commitment to the truth, we have to show our children that words have meaning—by doing what we say and by saying what we do. Moreover, we must begin by believing our children, so they can begin telling the truth. Here's how it went for Rebecca, whose daughter Violet, seven, had told her mother that the babysitter hit her little brother. Rebecca immediately fired the sitter, telling Violet, "You see, I believe what you tell me, and there are consequences." So when the following week, Violet told her something about the new babysitter, Rebecca asked, "Are you sure?" and Violet immediately changed her story, "No, it was just nonsense!"

Indeed, setting an example for our children also means treating them the way we would like them to treat others. If we are kind and respectful toward them, they will in turn mimic us and act the same with their friends, their own children, and all those around them.

## Knowledge

In order to convey our values to our children, we also ought to transmit our knowledge, so they become able to think and understand how the world works, which they pick up on more quickly than we might think.

While walking down the street with her five-year-old son, Dimitri, Laura noticed a child seated in the front seat of a car without wearing his seat belt. Laura exclaimed, "Parents like that should have their children taken away from them!" To which Dimitri replied, "They could start by taking their driver's license away."

It really is critical to discuss everything with our children: politics, literature, history, economics, botany, art, as well as the lives of our neighbors, while tailoring our explanations in accordance with our children's age and abilities, in order to teach them to observe, analyze, and reflect. For this to work, we need to be fully aware of where our children stand—the stage of their emotional and intellectual development—which we can only measure if we actually watch and listen to them. So here again, the way to go isn't to lecture our children, but to stay nearby when they watch the news or while they look things up on the Internet, and ask them their opinion on any subject, even if they lack the necessary knowledge to have a relevant thought—they will eventually have one after a few years of discussion. Indeed, as our children grow up, their field of interest widens. They ask questions about current events or things around them. So we need only follow their lead by giving them answers about the topics they genuinely take an interest in, and by continuing to tailor our explanations of the world and its complexities according to their age. It is out of the question for us to give them an edited version of reality since doing so only warps their reasoning. They need to be told about the dangers of the Internet, unemployment, addiction, violence, AIDS, pedophilia... It's the best way for them to understand the world around them and mature. When we complain about our children's lack of maturity, we can only blame ourselves; they would be more mature if we had just talked to them.

## The Keys to Connecting With Others

We also have to give our children the necessary tools to evolve in the world without us, which entails reaching out to others and being appreciated by them. First, because isolation and a lack of interest in others are nothing other than symptoms of suffering or illness. And second, it is a healthy, normal characteristic of human nature to connect with others. Social aptitude is therefore something that we should value and wish for our children, especially as it always comes easy to children who are balanced, generous, and respectful toward others. Having sharpened their minds in our company, they will hopefully have developed all sorts of skills and abilities, such as good judgment, or a great sense of humor, rendering them popular among their peers, and later helping them find their place and contribute to society.

For our children to reach out to and connect with others, though, they must be capable of understanding other human beings, and be able to put themselves in others' shoes. To this end, we should teach them to identify and analyze their own emotions, as well as those of the people around them.

Take the case of Avery, age six, who told his mother about what happened to him after school one day. He and some friends were taken to McDonald's by his babysitter. This in itself was a special event since Avery was allowed to go only on rare occasions. But he was upset with his babysitter, and when it came time to order he said, "I don't want anything" in the hope of provoking a strong reaction from her. But Avery's response didn't register with his babysitter, who was instructed never to force the boy to eat. So she replied, "Okay, fine," then proceeded to take the other children's orders. This frustrated Avery, who later confided in his mother, "I wanted a Big Mac." To which his mother answered, "See the lesson behind this: when you want to annoy others, you'd better be careful that you don't end up annoying yourself."

Similarly, for our children to be able to make the connection between their feelings and those of the people around them and ultimately be capable of empathy, we should talk to our children on a daily basis about the people they come across and discuss their feelings. It could be anyone and anything: a cashier's frustration over rude customers, a family friend grieving a loss, or the bitterness of an old, cranky aunt. It is essential that we avoid painting an artificial picture of the people and situations in our children's life in the process—however well intended it may seem—since it could ultimately be very misleading and give them a truncated view of reality. Many of us today cave in to the prevailing misconception that what's best is presenting our children with notions of how the world ought to be, rather than how it is, disregarding what's negative or reprehensible in the hope of transmitting a model of moral and positive behavior.

This is certainly what happens with parents and at schools that force children to invite all of their classmates to their birthday party—even those they don't like—as soon as they want to invite more than three or four people. The underlying message of this rule is that children are supposed to like everyone, which is disastrous. In enforcing this rule, parents forget to teach their children the most important idea: they are not obligated to like everyone, but instead to respect everyone. And by denying the fundamental principle of enmity, these adults force children to adopt a fake friendly behavior that requires them to repress their aggressive impulses, which, kept under wraps, can only become explosive, whereas they could have easily dissipated if they had been taken into account from the start.

Children perfectly understand likes and dislikes, and diplomatic problems; if this isn't already the case, their life in school, by virtue of daily interaction with peers, teaches them that feelings of rejection are an integral part of life. It is indispensable for us to explore these matters with our children in order to help them distinguish right from wrong in terms of behavior, teach them the ways to express their disagreement, and impart the nuances of differing opinions and arguments versus aggression and bullying.

For example, eight-year-old Enzo was invited to Alexa's house for the weekend. From Enzo's point of view, everything went very well. Yet Enzo was not invited to Alexa's birthday party the following weekend. Enzo approached Alexa to ask why, to which Alexa replied that Tamara—her best friend, who did not like Enzo—had told her that if he came, she would not. Therefore, Alexa chose to favor Tamara since she was her best friend. After hearing all that, Enzo replied, "Oh, okay! Now I get it. I just wanted to understand why." Whether or not Alexa was right to let Tamara dictate her guest list, Enzo was completely satisfied with her explanation and respected her decision.

Likewise, we should disregard the current injunction not to inform our children of our differences of opinion with our significant other so as to present a "united front," since our children are quite capable of understanding that we may have different views. A mother can say to her children: "I do not agree with your dad, who believes you have to go to church, but since it's important to him, you're going to go." She can also tell them: "I do not agree with the punishment your father gave you, so I will talk to him." Furthermore, seeing us interact when we disagree with the other parent teaches our children how to deal with someone with a differing opinion than theirs, and how to defend their ideas when necessary. Above all, it's essential for our children to see for themselves that if we believe the other parent is treating them unfairly, we will say so openly and stand up for them.

This approach also applies if we don't get along with the other parent, even after divorce. Our children need to have their feelings validated. While we shouldn't vent by saying horrible things about our former spouse and delight in making our children lose respect for one of their parents; it's a mistake to believe we are protecting our children by refraining from telling them the truth. One example might be masking the truth that their dad isn't paying child support or hiding that he isn't interested in seeing them or taking them on vacation, or that their mother is behaving badly. Our children sense the truth while they might not be certain of it, and may therefore not know if they have the right to feel distressed about it. For us to confirm they aren't mistaken amounts to validating how they feel. It allows them to understand that it's their father's or mother's problem and not their own, which gives them a chance to face the facts with more ease. So telling our children the truth about us is always liberating for them, because concealing the truth doesn't spare their pain; it just makes it more difficult for them to articulate and understand it.

That said, to be able to explain a difficult situation to our children, we must first analyze it ourselves and thus exercise our own critical thinking. This entails being willing to go against a common trend that generally finds it reprehensible to judge anyone or any situation in the name of not being offensive. This idea requires us to have a detachment that has nothing to do with high mindedness and generally results in blank indifference, because we end up losing interest in situations we are not supposed to judge or criticize. Refraining from judgment in this way also deprives our children of the valuable lessons we could have taught them on how to analyze and discern—judging character and situations is a skill they will most certainly need!

## ADVISING AND PROTECTING

Our children need consistent proof of our unconditional benevolence toward them, which we can provide by advising and defending them, as a lawyer would do. That means standing by them regardless of the situation, without excusing or overwhelming them when they do something wrong, as well as imposing strict rules of integrity on ourselves in order to demonstrate, in concrete ways, our loyalty to our children.

Take the example of Faith: after her son Landon broke up with Cadence, Faith remained in touch with Cadence, unaware that she was implicitly siding with her son's ex by choosing to continue sympathizing with the young woman. Though Faith may have sincerely liked Cadence, she was effectively prioritizing her own pleasure over the potential resentment of her son, who could easily view his mother's behavior as a betrayal.

No doubt that by doing so, Faith was boosting her ego, since the relationship she maintained with Cadence made her feel young and cool. But she did it at her son's expense and by getting in the middle of a relationship in which she didn't belong. Worst of all, this friendship was a way for Faith to outdo Landon and demonstrate she had managed to maintain a good relationship with Cadence, whereas her son could not.

Being loyal to Landon would require cutting ties with Cadence, or at the very least informing Landon whenever she was planning on seeing his ex-girlfriend. The same loyalty is required of us if it is one of our friends who misbehaves with our children.

This was the case for Ophelia, who one day phoned Maddox, a painter friend of her parents, as she wanted to give them one of his paintings as a twentieth wedding anniversary present. But Maddox was unbelievably discourteous, telling Ophelia she ought to address herself to his gallery and made it clear it wasn't worth calling him directly if she didn't have the money to pay for one of his pieces—a brutal and unnecessary remark coming from an intimate family friend. Ophelia recounted the incident to her parents, but they listened distractedly and continued to invite Maddox over regularly without realizing that they were thus siding with their friend over their daughter, who took this as proof of their indifference toward her.

## On Their Peer Relationships

Ideally, our children can manage without us intervening. But in order for this to happen, our children must be able to count on our advice regarding what they are going through, notably with their peers, and to consult us on matters such as violence in school, popularity, jealousy, or harassment. For them to become independent, we have to teach them how to defend themselves by giving them a course of action to avoid being pushed around while still being fair with their peers, with advice such as: "Don't hit anyone smaller than you, but do respond to anyone your age who attacks you, and anyone bigger you can send to me." Or our lessons could include concocting comebacks our children could use against potential aggressors without putting themselves at fault by using violence. Such discussions are all the more important to have because they give our children the opportunity to talk to us about difficult situations that they may be experiencing but tend to want to keep to themselves, both out of shame and because they don't want us to worry. By discussing these matters with them, we help our children open up sooner about potential bullying or violence and help prevent things from degenerating further.

Teaching our children how to defend themselves is particularly important because they can't engage with others and socialize with their peers if they don't know how to oppose them verbally or physically when things go wrong.

If, on the other hand, our children cannot cope with a problem on their own and ask us for help, we must intervene. But we need to react in proportion to the gravity of our children's situation and suffering. For example, if a classmate broke our child's tooth, it makes no sense for us to blow things out of proportion by humiliating the guilty child and reporting him or her to the school officials as if he or she committed some felony crime. But if the situation is serious, such as a pattern of bullying, and is causing profound or repeated suffering to our child, there is a risk of real danger and we should take strong action. To name just a few examples of properly proportioned responses, we could go to see the aggressor's parents to alert them to their child's behavior, and threaten to sue them if they fail to act upon it, or we could go to the school to talk to our child's teacher or the principal, or, if possible, enroll our child in a different school. No matter what course we take, it is imperative that we display a force that reassures our children. We must convey the image of being strong and determined, without showing any concern that our actions might worsen the situation, without dillydallying, without thinking too much or being too polite, and without appearing to find the situation complicated. In short, we must show our children we are vehemently defending them so that they understand they can stop being afraid.

### Against the Other Parent

The same intransigence is required from us if our children are victims of verbal, physical, or moral abuse from our partner, whether it is their parent or stepparent. In such cases, even if we begin by stating our disagreement to our spouse privately to try to convince him or her to change their behavior, we should also oppose his or her bad behavior openly in front of our children, who need to see for themselves that we are standing by them and defending them. But we shouldn't stop there, since doing nothing more than that, in the name of parental unity, nevertheless amounts to giving our partner's misconduct a stamp of approval. Playing both sides only ends up sabotaging our behavior toward our children.

Indeed, with these half measures, we focus on protecting and defending our children from our partner instead of actually raising and educating them. We attempt to excuse or explain our partner's behavior to our children, all the while doing our best to comfort them and compensate for the violence they suffer by, for example, creating happy moments for them. But this leads us to refrain from disciplining them when they misbehave, by fear that our scolding, although justified, would only add fuel to the fire, and cause even more suffering than what they already cope with. We can't educate and fix at the same time. Consequently, our duty to our children is not about trying to make things better within the dysfunctional family circle, but rather to provide them with a clearly delineated safe and quiet space where they can breathe, develop themselves, and benefit from a real upbringing, instead of our simple, damage-repairing goodwill. In other words, we should separate from our partner for our children's sake, and—depending on the circumstances—request sole custody of our children or establish some sort of joint custody that will at least reduce their exposure to our partner's violence. It will offer them an alternative place to live, in which they can find refuge and the strength to nevertheless maintain a relationship with the toxic parent.

## Against Institutions

We also need to represent and defend our children against institutions because we are the only ones who can do it. This role may entail advocating for our children when their school has wrongly accused them of bullying, or righting some other injustice of which they are the target.

For Angela, it meant defending her son Owen against their building's super, who claimed Owen had bumped into an old lady in the stairwell without apologizing. Angela confronted Owen, who told her that it wasn't him, but gave her the name of a likely culprit. Angela then returned to the super and asked him to apologize to Owen for wrongly accusing him, which the super did. It was only fair, since Angela would have certainly required Owen to apologize to the old lady if he had been guilty.

Our duty to defend and protect our children also means being fierce advocates for them when they are in the hospital. Take Beatrice, whose five-year-old daughter, Oriana, was hospitalized for two days to remove her tonsils. When Beatrice was told that it was forbidden for parents to stay overnight in the hospital room with their children, she refused to acquiesce to the nurses who advised Beatrice to tell Oriana it wasn't a big deal to stay on her own, because she was a big girl. Instead, Beatrice reassured Oriana that she would leave as late as possible and would return as early as possible, when Oriana would still be asleep.

Communicating, transmitting values, knowledge and experience, reading emotions, teaching empathy, counseling and defending—just listing the different aspects of our role as parents is enough to see how important it is that parenting be our main focus, and how rich the bond created with our children has to be. And this job needs to be maintained no matter much competition we face in our modern world; social networks, for instance, should be a basis for conversation rather than a source of distance between our children and us.

# 9

✎

# Giving Up Our
# Need for Control

*What's sadder than children who leave?*
*Children who stay!*

—DANIEL PENNAC, *Family Life*, 1993

It took me a long time to understand that my cheer-
leader approach to my children, an approach I thought
was vital to their personal confidence, in fact resulted
in the exact opposite of the desired result. In reality it
was a coping mechanism to stop me from being afraid.
Afraid of what? Of what might happen to them? Of their
pain or failure? These questions are precisely what my
constant encouragement prevented me from exploring,
because the fine words I spoke to my children fulfilled
the function of mantras, forever brushing aside my own
anxiety. But this precautionary enthusiasm stood in the
way of my feeling *genuine* enthusiasm. In addition, my
constant nervous insistence to my children—"you're fantastic," "you can do it"—had the double disadvantage of
failing to convince them and preventing me from seeing
them honestly and without preconception, which would,

of course, have allowed me to see their weaknesses, but also their strengths.

I know that I'm not alone in having misinterpreted my roles and duties as a parent. So many of us believe we need to interfere in our children's lives in order to control them. In reality, it is essential that, while being present and supportive, we also keep our distance. Leaving them to make their own way would have allowed me to watch them overcome their difficulties and would have given me confidence in them. Instead, I let myself get caught up in the spiral of false kindnesses based on the unconscious conviction that my children were incapable of coping without me. This conviction inevitably meant I wanted to do things for them, as helicopter parents do all over the world, but particularly in the United States, where most people see this behavior as a positive, and mistake parental control and intervention for true care and an appreciation of responsibilities, and where conversely a parent's withdrawal from his or her children's lives is viewed as negligence.

An extreme example of interference is seen in the reality show *Keeping Up with the Kardashians*, which offers its viewers the illusion of behind-the-scenes glimpses of the family's tribulations and frivolous daily life. Conceived and led by the matriarch, the show captures a mother who actually created a business model in which her children embody the roles she assigns to them as she manages their careers, their marriages, and their ambitions. Despite the obvious horror of this situation, the Kardashian sisters have become role models for millions of viewers.

## AVOIDING BEING OVERLY SUPPORTIVE

The first mistake we parents make? Thinking it's our responsibility to infuse our children with happiness and self-confidence and believing that we will achieve this through love and benevolence. It's never going to happen. Happiness and self-esteem are not things that can be handed out like treats. It is utterly useless for us to flood our children with continuous waves of encouragement and praise for no tangible reason, against the sense of obligation many of us feel to do so. We hope, in vain, that our words will eventually lead them to blossom to the point of feeling like the eighth wonder of the world.

What we don't account for with these well-meaning but artificial encouragements is how our children will inevitably be treated when they are at the mercy of the outside world, where jibes about all types of shortcomings—for instance if our children are overweight, smaller than their peers, or lousy students—are commonplace. Our children are bound to be confused by such a sharp disconnect between our praise and the criticisms they encounter outside the home. They may therefore conclude one of two things: either our enthusiasm is forced, and conveys our pity and a lack of confidence in them, which leads our children to feel like losers; or else our enthusiasm is sincere and a product of our blindness and ignorance of their imperfections, which gives our children the feeling of being unworthy of our praise, and thus of being impostors.

In the latter cases, our children's confusion also increases because it seems impossible to them that we, who in their eyes have so much authority, could be completely wrong when we tell them they are fantastic. So they don't know if they should trust what they feel or what they hear from us. This causes our children such unease that it often brings them to try to juggle both perspectives, by oscillating between an inferiority and superiority complex—a state quite far from the confidence we had hoped to infuse them with at the outset.

What are we to make of all this, if our actions lead our children to be either doubtful or conceited and pretentious? How can we give our children self-confidence? Well, we can't, because we don't have that power. Our duty is limited to trying to create the conditions that will enable our children to acquire self-confidence for themselves.

To become self-confident, our children must overcome challenges on their own. Our role is to help them do so without sugar-coating their circumstances, and to guide them toward solutions or plans of action, by acknowledging their problems and flaws, while at the same time putting them into perspective. For example, if our child is overweight, we might say: "Yes, you're too heavy, and people can be cruel about it. But being overweight is not who you are, you're much more than that." Or, if our child is performing poorly in school, we could say: "Yes, you're a bad student, but you are not a dummy. And I'll do what I can to help you when you decide that you want to improve your grades."

Such honesty may seem brutal, even cruel. But when it comes from a place of tenderness, it soothes our children, reassuring them that we love them no matter what, even as we recognize their flaws. Our role as parents should thus be limited to being supportive of our children through the good and the bad by using honesty as a springboard to enable them to overcome their challenges by themselves.

## LETTING THEM FIND THEIR OWN WAY

Overcoming challenges on their own is so beneficial to children that it is essential we refrain from interfering in their lives by sparing them difficulties or smoothing them out on their behalf.

### Letting Them Do Things for Themselves

This starts with not doing things for them at any stage of their development: when they are babies, let them crawl to the object they want rather than hand it to them; when they are toddlers, have them dress on their own rather than doing it to speed things up; and when they are teenagers, don't do their homework for them. Letting them do things for themselves may often turn out to be tedious, time-consuming, or boring, but it actually amounts to sending our children the message that we believe they are capable of taking care of things for themselves, which is crucial; they won't even try standing on their own two feet unless they believe we think they can.

Without too much thought, Stephanie asked her six-year-old son Peter to run into the pharmacy and buy Children's Tylenol suppositories while she double-parked the car. She immediately realized that Peter panicked at her request, but since she had already asked, she decided to go through with it without giving into the temptation of getting the job done more efficiently herself (although she was in a rush, which was why she had double-parked in the first place). So she decided to be patient with Peter, who could not remember the name Tylenol or understand the notion of a suppository or children's medication. As a result, he ended up going back and forth between the pharmacy and the car several times to get her to repeat the complicated words. And she did just that, aware of how crucial it was for Peter to overcome his fear, in order for him to prove to himself that he could do it. His triumphant smile as he left the pharmacy for the last time with the mission accomplished proved her right.

Similarly, we need to let our children decide when they choose to try something new and when they choose to regress. It's pointless to alarm ourselves if we see them doing so. For example, we should oblige if our child wants a baby bottle at night when they have outgrown the habit, or if they suddenly refuse to walk so that we pick them up in our arms again, or if, on the contrary, they don't want to be carried anymore. Indeed, it is up to our children to decide on their development. It is up to them to shape us as parents, and not up to us parents to shape them. Loving our children isn't about controlling or bossing them around.

## Letting Them Experience Hardships

Letting our children figure things out on their own means we have to let them struggle and feel pain. Franny sent her son Nicolas, eight, to summer camp. After a few very unhappy days, Nicolas asked if he could cut the camp short and come home. Franny was very tempted to go pick him up, but changed her mind when she realized that, far from protecting Nicolas, letting her son come home as soon as he asked would send him the signal that he was weak and unable to survive in an environment he didn't like. So, if the camp was to last for only one week, Franny should tell Nicolas, "Hold on until the end, I know you can do it. However, I promise that I will never send you to camp again because you obviously don't like it." That way Nicolas ends up feeling he overcame the challenge. And if the camp was to last three weeks, the best thing would be to try to buy some time by saying, "Stay a couple days and if you still really don't like it, we'll reassess the situation," allowing Nicolas to get something positive out of an unpleasant experience by drawing some pride from the fact he was able to endure it an honorable number of days.

## Letting Them Experience the Consequences of Their Actions

Letting our children figure things out on their own requires that we sit back and let them experience the consequences of their actions. Indeed, when we intervene and say, "Don't worry, I'm here, I'll get you out of the mess you got yourself into," we only reassure ourselves by strengthening our power as the parent, to the detriment of our children. In doing so, we prevent them from getting out of sticky situations on their own and potentially succeeding at something difficult, which would instead teach them to rely on themselves before relying on us, and enable them to feel capable of taking charge of their lives.

In the same way, our interference, which keeps our children from suffering the consequences of their actions, also prevents them from understanding they are the ones shaping their future, and that their actions are ultimately their problem. As a result, we must step back as soon as possible to empower our children, and this is far more challenging and constructive than fixing their mistakes.

Consider Louise's son, James, who, after repeating his last year of middle school, got even worse grades than the previous year. As the time to graduate approached, a family friend worried, "What do you plan on doing next year?" And James answered, "I'm not worried. My mom will find a solution." Having overheard this, Louise realized she had been in the wrong, and obviously overprotective of her son and overly efficient in solving his problems.

She decided not to help, despite the consequences. She was aware that if she didn't intervene, her son would likely be sent to a high school that wasn't geared toward his academic interest, which was science. Louise refrained from looking at private schools as an alternative solution. In September, after a summer of uncertainty about where he would end up and just two days before school started, James learned that his only option was a vocational high school. Meanwhile, his younger brother, Christopher, was about to start sixth grade at a science magnet school. James did not say a word for two weeks.

One day, while accompanying Louise to pick up Christopher from school, James ran into one of his friends who had started high school in the same school as his younger brother. The friend couldn't believe it when he learned what school James was attending. That same evening, James told his mother, "Get me out of there." She replied, "I can't, not with your poor science grades. If you have a good report card by January, I will try then to plead your case to the director of Christopher's school." Two days later, she went to Christopher's orientation meeting, but did not discuss James's situation.

But James, unable to imagine that his mother would not attempt the impossible for him, asked upon her return, "So did you try to get me in?" "No," she answered. The following day, again, James became more insistent, "Do something. I'm not cut out for carpentry and welding, and I can't stay there."

At that point Louise asked for a meeting with the principal of Christopher's school, and when she met with the principal, she spoke only the truth, including the fact that James didn't do any work. By miracle, the principal decided to give James a second chance, warning him that he would be expelled if his grades stayed the same. From then on, James's grades improved dramatically—but only because Louise had let him suffer the shock of reality. She had let him experience the anxiety of not knowing which school he would end up attending, which lasted the entire summer vacation, because the admission office sent no update— additionally, at the beginning of the new academic year, she had let him agonize for the first two weeks at the vocational school. That way, she gave James the opportunity to seize the second chance he was given, which he then took advantage of for the rest of his academic life.

# THE HIGH STAKES OF INDEPENDENCE

The second mistake we parents make? Believing that it's up to us to control our children's development and to decide how and when to grant them their independence. Once again, that's not the case. Independence is something all children aspire to, and we need to support this by letting them determine when and how they want to achieve it. We must content ourselves with being at their side throughout their upbringing, at first physically and later symbolically, to reassure them and allow them to reach their goal.

This is a theme present in the life of J.M. Barrie, the Scottish author of *Peter Pan*. At age six, he lost his brother, his mother's favorite child. Barrie's childhood was based on this family tragedy and he spent his whole life trying to fill the void left in his mother's heart. No wonder that, being unable to reach adult autonomy, which is only possible with the reassuring presence of a mother, he would write *The Adventures of Peter Pan*, situated in a land where children are immortal, never grow up, and aren't subject to adult rules. Barrie's universe inspired what is called Peter Pan Syndrome, from which the singer Michael Jackson is said to have suffered, and unapologetically too, since he named his ranch Neverland, after the imaginary world in Barrie's story.

Nevertheless, letting our children gain their independence at their own pace is substantially harder for us than controlling the process. Our children's desire for independence often surfaces at times or in ways that are disconcerting or unpleasant for us. It can show up very early on, even at four years old, when they might refuse to tell us what's wrong with them as a sign that they are unhappy with our meddling in their lives.

Their thirst for independence can also result in lies our children tell to resist and retaliate against our intrusion. In those instances, we need to accept our children's behavior without scolding them, as long as their reactions—whether a rejection of our input or lying—don't cause them any harm. For example, when Lena's son came home with toys stolen from school falling out of his pockets, she simply responded by saying, "It's okay, we'll return them tomorrow."

Most of the time, our children's demand for autonomy is manifested during adolescence, giving rise to the infamous "adolescent crisis." This often has less to do with our children, who have every right to emancipate themselves, than with us, who struggle so much to relinquish our control that we impose irrational and sometimes unjust rules on our children. This was the case with Stella, who let Emily, her sixteen-year-old daughter, go to a party, but gave her an illogical and arbitrary curfew that she was expected to meet no matter how she got home. These rules chiefly revealed Stella's reluctance to relinquish parental power. Indeed, what was dangerous for Emily was to come home alone in the dark, not to come home late. Stella would have been wiser to let Emily come home at the time of her choice, but ask that she do so by taking a taxi or that she be accompanied by someone trustworthy.

Our children's emancipation causes us major discomfort. This discomfort takes the form of concern, which grows over time depending on our children's age and the extent of their issues. Our concern may very well appear legitimate, but we mostly use it as an excuse to pry into our children's lives, asking them to touch base and give updates at all times, either with old-fashioned nosy questions, or via text message, or any kind of technological apps that now allow us to track and monitor our children.

However, even though it's inevitable, our concern doesn't justify our intrusiveness; on the contrary, we should be releasing our control so that our children gain independence. As a rule, we should probably grant our children the independence they ask for. It can be fairly easy, for example, if they ask to go away with friends for the weekend, but it can also cause us great anxiety.

Chelsea's fourteen-year-old son, Adam, asked if he could get a Vespa. Given the choice to either accept, refuse, or defer her son's request until he was older, Chelsea at first refused. But when Adam turned sixteen, Chelsea agreed and explained her reasoning: "If I say no, it would only be to reassure myself. I would therefore be thinking of me, and not of you. So I will make an effort. But I'll ask you to make an effort as well, namely not driving at night because that would terrify me." Adam first thanked Chelsea for her honesty and fairness, and then gave his promise and kept his word.

But granting our children the independence they ask for may prove even more complicated if, for example, our children are already leaning toward delinquent behaviors. In such instances, it's clear that if we give them extra freedom, they will act even more recklessly before succeeding at reasoning on their own, and we may not be willing to take that risk.

However, we can rest assured to a greater extent than we might think; if we have been attentive and supportive of our children all along, there's a good chance that—despite their desire to differentiate themselves from us—they will come back to us. Perhaps not on the straight and narrow path, but on one that is both suitable to them and compatible with the values and culture we have infused them with. Furthermore, we should keep in mind that we would be taking a greater risk by not giving our children their independence, and suffering their lack of it further down the road.

Let's take Cate's experience. She worried about her niece Jenna, her sister Brooklyn's daughter, who, at thirty-nine, was still living with her mother. One day Cate took the bull by the horns and told Jenna it was high time she moved out. She also offered to help finance the purchase of an apartment, while suggesting it was better not to discuss any of this with Brooklyn as she'd likely not take it well. Cate knew how possessive Brooklyn was of her daughter, and she didn't want to start a fight with her sister. But Jenna went right ahead and told her mother everything, and Brooklyn immediately got upset at her sister's interference since she wanted to keep Jenna to herself, without a second's reflection about what might be in Jenna's best interest.

Cate could not understand why Jenna rushed to repeat their conversation to Brooklyn and why she could not accept her aunt's generous offer. But it was perfectly logical that Jenna would reveal everything to her mother, since she was unable to disobey her in any way. Had she been able to, she would have already moved out. By sharing her aunt's proposal with Brooklyn, Jenna was essentially testing the idea of leaving her and asking for her permission to do so. Even though Jenna was thirty-nine years old, her emotional maturity was that of a ten- or twelve-year-old. However, unlike a child that develops and grows naturally, it was difficult for Jenna to satisfy her need for independence at a later age, since that potential in her, like an immobilized limb, had weakened to the point of atrophy. Therefore, it was pointless for Cate to present Jenna with solutions to move out of her mother's home because Jenna had grown incapable of living without her mother, whose approval she constantly begged for and would always rely on.

The tragedy that befalls parents like Brooklyn, who prevent their children from gaining independence, is inevitable: when they ultimately find their adult children too cumbersome and feel ready to have them move on, they discover they've stunted any chance their children may have of doing so and living their own lives.

## IT'S UP TO OUR CHILDREN TO SHAPE US AS PARENTS, AND NOT THE OTHER WAY AROUND

The third mistake we parents make? Believing that we are helping our children by interfering in their lives. This belief seems legitimate to us since we feel that we have the experience and tenderness required to do so. We therefore have no qualms about controlling our children's lives, including weighing in when they make their own decisions.

In the 2013 movie *Les garçons et Guillaume, à table!* (*Me, Myself and Mum*), Guillaume Gallienne describes his childhood growing up in an upper-class family. From birth, his mother, who already had two boys but longed to have a little girl, treats Guillaume like the daughter she never had. Guillaume willingly plays this role because he is fascinated by his mother and wants to resemble her, dress like her, and imitate her voice and all her gestures. And he is so good at playing this role that he's persuaded he is a girl, and those around him all think he's gay. So, when he meets Amandine and announces his plans to marry her, his mother is very surprised, almost disappointed, that her "favorite daughter" could possibly love a woman other than her. But Guillaume is able to reassure her because it's thanks to his mother that he loves women.

## Refraining from Interfering in Their Lives

### *Not Influencing Their Choices*

Here again, it's up to our children to "shape" us as parents, and not up to us to "shape" our children according to our preconceived notions, however well intentioned. Children who take the initiative to express their needs, desires, and expectations give us the opportunity to be good parents by processing them in real time while keeping their best interest in mind.

As a result, much like teachers, they guide us and shape us as parents. But those of us who dump our values, knowledge, beliefs, and opinions onto our children when we see fit, demanding that they conform to us in all things, are most likely crushing their inner rhythm or their personality. First, because we have so much power over them that any input of ours amounts to dictating their conduct. Second, because, despite what we may think, we are not the greatest judges of what best suits our children. For example, when it comes to future jobs and careers, we usually push our children to choose financial security and stability, or to reproduce what is familiar to us, directly or indirectly, by saying: "Do as I do" or "Do what we do in this family," which seems perfectly legitimate to us since our advice is grounded in our values and traditions. However, the path we set them on is often narrow and limited: we might see our children as doctors, financial advisors, or insurers, but not as landscapers, cabinet-makers, artists, or video game designers, as children might choose to be if they decided on their own. Furthermore, we can be wrong, since we are hardly experts in all fields. We may also use inappropriate or outdated reasoning by saying "Do this or do that" without realizing that our errors in judgment can have serious consequences for our children.

Faith, a graduate from a prestigious French university, wanted her daughter, Amelia, to attend a competitive college as she had, but in the United States instead, a country she considered more conducive to success than France. Faith pushed Amelia well beyond what was reasonable and respectful in order to get her daughter to apply to the best

American universities. But in the end the bright Amelia didn't get into any of them, which was devastating for her and left her with a very severe and destructive feeling of failure. What went wrong? Faith, who had indeed made sure Amelia had the excellent academic record required in France, thought she knew the admissions criteria of American universities. But Faith never did any research into them and was actually very uninformed. So she had not taken into account the importance American schools give to an applicant's emotional development, personality, and extracurricular activities.

Finally, we do not realize that putting pressure on our children to conform to our expectations is no different than trampling them. Indeed, as soon as we push for a certain academic or professional track, we force our children to deny their own desires to accommodate ours by using them as trophies or honor badges, crippling them emotionally in the process. And this disequilibrium will cause them trouble later in their adult lives.

Boris, a French student at the Polytechnique school, had been repeatedly beaten by his father and harassed about his grades so he'd be accepted into a top university. From the moment he had graduated, he was always hired right after being interviewed for jobs, but was invariably fired soon after because he couldn't help but sabotage himself. For example, Boris was sent out of state by his employer for two months in order to study and analyze the company's operations, and write up a detailed report with his recommendations. However, he sent it only two days later in an intelligent but inappropriately concise email, which got him fired on the spot.

Such was also the case with Skyla, whose mother had pushed her into the acting career that she hadn't been able to achieve herself. Skyla, who could neither express her own desire nor her own vocation, obeyed her mother's wishes and achieved the success her mother had not, only to become her mother's substitute rather than her own person.

## Not Labeling Them

We are even capable of causing our children great distress by expecting from them daily behaviors that, unbeknownst to us, make them suffer. This is what happens when we project onto them an image that pleases, appeases, or valorizes us—such as that of an egghead or the family clown.

Indeed, this controlling behavior translates in our being more interested in their image than who they really are, leaving them with no choice than to follow our implicit orders in order to avoid being ignored or rejected. And as children, they cannot take the risk. Thus, they try to obey us and give up their own personality, possibly their own destiny.

In *La Promesse de l'aube* (*Promise at Dawn*), Romain Gary's fictionalized autobiography published in 1960, the grown-up narrator describes the exuberant love that his mother, an eccentric former actress, has for him. Single and overbearing, she envisions an exceptional life for her son, and encourages him constantly, never doubting his glorious future. After failing at various artistic endeavors, he finally fulfills her wishes by finding his talent in writing—an area where he can be a magnificent liar. Ultimately, he commits suicide, once he has completed his work and the success his mother wanted so much for him was attained.

Such children suffer from the fact that their parents don't really know them. For example, if they aren't really as happy as they are expected to act, then they can hardly know who they are beyond the role that they have been compelled to play. Their fear of disappointing their parents inevitably leads them to cheat themselves. They banish the slightest moment of sadness, or they clown even if they are feeling down, burying their pain, which eventually resurfaces in one way or another; usually psychosomatically, in the form of asthma or hives, or any other physical symptom of anxiety.[13] Alternatively, when assigned the role of "good student," children trying to live up to their parents' academic expectations will depreciate themselves if they fail, sometimes going as far as sinking into depression or harming themselves in some way, in order to cloud or spoil the unattainable image projected onto them.

In *Mars*, an autobiographical book written by thirty-two-year-old Fritz Zorn after discovering he has cancer, the author suddenly realizes his illness was caused by his bourgeois upbringing in the wealthiest neighborhood of Zurich, an upbringing he considers "cancerous" to the point of having been "brought up to die." He lived his life through others without the ability to express his own feelings. Alone and depressed, he experienced neither friendship nor love. His cancer, he thinks, is the best idea he's come up with, in order to commit slow suicide without having to take the responsibility. He learns of the publishing of his literary testimony the day he dies.

## The Toxic Effects of Hovering

Parents' dominance is sometimes so harmful to children that it can only end in disaster. Either it provokes an earthquake in the family when a child attempts to destroy the fake self their parents have imposed on them, usually during adolescence, or parents consider their job as caretakers and educators to have been successfully accomplished, irrespective of their child's well-being and opinion. Indeed, just like bad engineers who produce a defective machine without ever questioning their method, parents might get what they wanted by molding their children into the model adults they designed, but they will have only succeeded in rendering their children docile, never understanding the negative effects of their child-rearing. These often surface much later or in ways they don't think to link to their parenting methods.

These children, victims of how they have been shaped emotionally by their parents, often experience secret sufferings or encounter problems that they hide or consider shameful, without being able to understand or even name them. They may suffer from isolation and loneliness, hopelessly protecting themselves by remaining emotionally detached from others, especially in their love life, and incapable of bonding with anyone. Or they may try to heal themselves by subduing and conquering partners who, as their parents had, demand they behave in ways that make them suffer.

This was the case for Alexandra, attracted to a serial playboy named Samuel who expected her to be loving, attentive, and solely focused on him and his well-being, while

not being able to stand it when she expressed her own suffering about his cheating. Samuel was essentially giving
Alexandra two choices: being abandoned if she showed her
real self, namely a woman who needed to be loved and have
her needs met, or suffer in silence if she wanted to stay with
him, which was indeed what she wanted because she hoped
one day to change and tame him. This was the same with
Igor, who only fell in love with married women who were
incapable of leaving their husbands and therefore incapable of choosing him. Ditto for the countless people who
marry someone who criticizes them and seeks to change
them—wanting them to be sophisticated when they're
only plain Janes, to love nature when they only like cities,
to be full-figured when they are skinny, to be good with
their hands when they are clumsy, down to earth when
they are intellectuals, and so on.

## Setting High Expectations

Renouncing interference in our children's lives does not
mean renouncing our role as parents. And it's out of the
question that we do so, because it is our job to give our children the means to fulfill their ambitions, and therefore to
help them succeed by making ambitious demands of them.
Academically speaking, this means encouraging our children to get the best education possible given their aptitudes
and personality, by adjusting our demands according to
what is easy or difficult for them—teachers being the most
objective judges of this—in order to push them without setting them up for failure by asking the impossible. But our
high expectations should also extend beyond the academic

world, since our demands ought to encourage our children to be accomplished in all areas of their lives, so they can become beautiful inside and out, and appreciated by those around them.

However, we need to be very careful not to confuse being demanding with being intrusive. For example, if it is important that our children feel attractive, in order to confidently engage with others, it would be disastrous for us to try to shape our children's body, wardrobe, or hair-style according to our own personal taste. The only way for us to express the justifiably high expectations that we have for them is to demand they be proud of themselves. This attitude, both ambitious and respectful, encourages children to succeed in all areas of their lives, which will make them happy, all the while preventing us from dictating them their behavior.

We can thus take on this balanced approach—ambition coupled with respect—at all stages of our children's lives because it retains its virtue from infancy right into adulthood. For example, Amber's son, Matteo, a young doctor fresh out of residency, was reluctant to take over a classmate's shift because he doubted his abilities, saying, "I don't know how to put in stitches." Amber felt she had to shake Matteo to help him overcome his fear, so she replied, "Your classmate knows the same stuff as you know. If you refuse to do this, you're just a wimp."

## Stepping Back and Chilling Out

Letting our children call the shots requires that we make a conscious effort to let go of any image that we have formed of them, as well as any preconceived idea of success we had in mind for them. It also requires we give up our efforts to tame what is not under our control or what worries us, and our attempts to eliminate all the surprises our children would inevitably spring on us if they had it their way. In short, we must stop trying to control our children in order to reassure ourselves.

### Accepting Their Screw-ups

We must admit that our children's paths are at times so painful for us to watch that many really cannot sit back and do so—in particular when we are convinced our children are ruining their youth, intelligence, or beauty, and we are afraid to see them missing out on their education or their love life at moments we consider crucial turning points in their lives. But we must begin by asking ourselves if what makes us suffer is our children's suffering, or seeing the preconceived image we had of them tarnished. In truth, we may be feeling more sorry for ourselves than for our children than we'd like to admit, and sometimes we betray that by saying "me, me, me," when we complain: "My daughter kept me up all night with an ear infection," or "How could he do this to me!" if our child is arrested for a DUI or hospitalized for attempted suicide.

Only once we rid ourselves of our parental ego will we understand that we are not the best judges of the right path for our children or their timing in life. Indeed, not everyone peaks at age eighteen; some children only blossom at forty. As for our children's screw-ups, we are not in a good position to blame them: when asked about our own lives, we readily admit to having made questionable choices, and that it is those choices, even the bad ones, that made us who we are.

It is only once we have understood that what we have in mind for our children will never amount to the right choice for them—even if we think it is correct and rational—that we can let our children choose their own path, find their way, and accept that they make their own mistakes. That is unless we feel we cannot support their behavior if, for example, they do drugs or if they stray into a particularly toxic relationship. In these cases we may choose to tell them, in the strongest terms, that we don't approve and that we prefer to pull away or cut ties with them in hopes of making them react. And it often works (especially if we otherwise have given our children space), since a child in a situation like this may have needed such a wake-up call in order to find their way back from the edge.

### Giving Adult Children Their Space

Unless we are experiencing serious health or financial crises, we ought to rejoice not being number one on our adult children's priority list, and celebrate the fact that they no longer need us, because this really is the ultimate accomplishment of our mission as parents. We should instead read our feelings of uselessness and dismissal as great victories, and not seek to offset our sadness by calling on our children, who need to build their lives outside our fold. It is important we find a new balance allowing us to continue our relationship with them by being present and available without hanging over their adult lives.

This means we refrain from insisting that our children visit by guilt-tripping them or by multiplying family obligations. But it also implies that we try to be interesting by reading, going to museums or the movies, and following the news, so our children want to talk to us. By doing so, we will be able to give them good advice that they find compelling and that truly educates and nurtures (but only if and when we are asked to do so), so they can turn to us if they need to, and we will be able to come up with fun and friendly family rituals so that they may be drawn to our home.

Finally, it also means we stop rehashing the inevitable mistakes we made as parents. After all, had we been perfect, our children would never have been capable of leaving home. However, if our relationship with our children suffered because of our past mistakes and we did hurt them, we need to recognize this and apologize to them, because children are by nature loving and indulgent toward their parents, and therefore, it is never too late to pacify and improve our relationship with them. After that, it will be up to our children, now adults, to do their work at healing their wounds so as not to pass them on to their own children.

# Conclusion

Only when adding the final touches to these lines did I wonder what kind of book I had written. An essay? A practical guide? Probably a bit of both. It is a book rooted in concrete situations that we may experience as parents—not so much to highlight our children's needs, like most how-to books out there, but rather to address the challenges we face as parents when we try to raise our children successfully.

What I describe here is the philosophy of parenting that I developed by trial and error as I worked through my own difficulties as a parent. I was indeed off to a rough start despite my eagerness and initial gut feeling that I would be a "good mother." I quickly lost confidence when I realized that I was doing exactly the opposite of what I had intended to do, and that I couldn't control my negative impulses toward my children. Discouraged, I swung back and forth between giving up and striving for perfection—ultimately zigzagging through a series of contradictory behaviors that are the exact contrary of the consistency needed in children's upbringing. All the while, I increasingly felt that being a "good mother" was an impossible task.

Then I realized that I had to react, work on myself, and develop the benchmarks I lacked as a parent. Looking back now, beyond the satisfaction of having completed this ambitious journey, I feel a sense of accomplishment. It was important for me to share these reflections in a book written with other parents in mind: a book for all those who, like me, feel they are having trouble raising their children or who doubt their instincts or abilities. My goal is to encourage such parents to take all the energy they usually waste in worrying and feeling guilty and redirect it toward their children. Ultimately, I hope to show that there is no need to be perfect parents in order to do a good job at raising their children, and that it is indeed possible to have a happy and respectful relationship with them.

# Acknowledgments

A special and grateful thanks to Yvonne Cárdenas, Elena Cicognani, Anna Condo, Eleonore Condo, Jon Delogu, Sophie Dimich-Louvet, Angèle Guillotte, Judith Gurewich, Catherine Krespine, Bonnie Nadzam, Caroline Weber.

I also owe a debt of gratitude to all the people who trusted me with their stories of parenting under the influence.

# PRACTICAL GUIDE

# 1

✎

# What Kind of Parent Are You?

## YOUR RELATIONSHIP TO YOUR OWN CHILDHOOD

1. **Reproducing the way your parents raised you is not a problem for you** because your childhood was happy and your parents wonderful. Raising your children is for you as exciting as is it natural. You are attentive, you keep your children's interests in mind, and you enjoy their company. In fact, you have a fantastic relationship with them, so much so that you don't understand the issues addressed in this book, which therefore isn't really of much interest to you.

2. **Reproducing the way your parents raised you is not a problem for you** because your childhood—if not happy—was uneventful. You have nothing for which to blame your parents. They did what they could (nobody is perfect and there is no miracle recipe for a perfect upbringing). Your relationship with your children? You do your best, but it's no picnic.

**Read:** The Unconscious Need to Prove Our Parents Right (p. 39); The Vicious Cycle (p. 41); Revisiting Our Childhood (p. 61); Acknowledging Abuse (p. 63); Detecting Covert Abuse (p. 68).

3. ***You do not reproduce the way your parents raised you*** since you raise your children by following your instincts, which are a product of your love for them, and can only be beneficial to them.

   **Read:** The Imprint of Childhood (p. 23); The Grip of Childhood: Parents Under the Influence (p. 26); The Power of Habit (p. 33).

4. ***There is no way you will reproduce how your parents raised you*** because you did not like your childhood. You've found the solution not to do so: your rule is to do the opposite of what your parents did so as not to inflict onto your children what you suffered during your childhood.

   **Read:** The Unconscious Need to Understand Our Childhood (p. 34); Doing the Opposite of Our Parents (p. 53).

5. ***You swore to yourself never to reproduce the way your parents raised you,*** but despite this, sometimes you find yourself doing to your children what made you suffer during your childhood. This conduct upsets you as much as it shames you.

**Read:** The Vicious Cycle (p. 41); Neutralizing Our Pain (p. 49); Correcting Our Behavior (p. 75).

6. ***You are constantly questioning what you do as a parent*** so as not to reproduce the way you were raised, but all these questions leave you unsure about which behavior to adopt with your children.

**Read:** Setting the Record Straight (p. 89); War and Peace (p. 141).

## YOUR RELATIONSHIP TO YOUR CHILDREN

1. ***You don't want to completely transform your life simply because you have children.*** You find that today's parents do way too much. What are daycares and babysitters there for anyway?

**Read:** Detecting Covert Abuse (p. 68); The Best Parents Thrive in Their Children's Company (p. 95); The Best Parents Make Their Children Their Number-One Priority (p. 99).

2. ***You are extremely strict with your children.*** For you, there is nothing quite like discipline. Otherwise kids run wild, just look at the disastrous results of permissive parenting!

**Read:** The Unconscious Need for Revenge (p. 43); Dead End Number One: Being Too Strict (p. 144).

3. **You are kind of permissive.** You think that, to be happy, children need to be loved, not disciplined. You encourage them constantly so they can feel good about themselves and be self-confident.

   **Read:** Dead End Number Two: Being Too Permissive (p. 150); Avoiding Being Overly Supportive (p. 200).

4. **You are very involved in your children's upbringing** because in today's competitive world, you believe it's your duty to raise high performing and accomplished individuals by organizing a schedule that you require they submit to.

   **Read:** Over-Supervising Our Children (p. 127); Free Range versus Helicopter Parenting (p. 128); How to Respect Their Need for Independence (p. 129); Picking Our Battles (p. 164); Bonding with Our Children (p. 176); Giving Up Our Need for Control (p. 198).

5. **You are extremely close to your children,** so much so that they are like friends and/or the sole purpose of your existence, and/or you spend all your time with them.

   **Read:** Detecting Covert Abuse (p. 68); Over-Supervising Our Children (p. 127); Free-Range versus Helicopter Parenting (p. 128); How to Respect Their Need for Independence (p. 129); Giving Up Our Need for Control (p. 198).

# 2

⤫

# Popular Beliefs

**We must shelter our children from our adult problems.**

FALSE. Children feel responsible for any problem they perceive to be hanging over us, and when their feelings don't coincide with our official story, they become so confused that they put their emotions aside or switch them off altogether to halt the suffering. They thereby deprive themselves, often for the rest of their lives, of an inner compass that is essential to their mental health and judgment (p. 19).

**The fact that siblings react differently to the same upbringing proves that our behavior as parents is less important than we think.**

FALSE. We just aren't aware of the degree to which we adopt a different attitude toward each of our children (pp. 12–13).

**Worrying is a sign of love.**

FALSE. Our concern as parents may well be inevitable, but it must be curbed because, by communicating our negative emotions, we push our children toward failure (pp. 13–19).

### Raising children is no picnic.

**FALSE.** On the contrary, our goal should be to experience enough pleasure in our children's company to engage in patient educational work with them (p. 19). Feeling pleasure in our children's company can be learned (pp. 95–99).

### We should trust our instincts.

**FALSE.** Indeed, if we did not have a happy childhood, we should instead be wary of our instincts because they lead us to yield to our unconscious automatic reflexes inherited from our past (p. 26).

### Children are by nature disobedient.

**FALSE.** It's exactly the opposite. Our children obey our conscious and unconscious desires (p. 13). In the long-term, they obey the image we have of them. So if we think they are liars or lazy, they will become so (p. 145).

### Children are ungrateful and rebellious.

**FALSE.** On the contrary, our children believe that we are always right, to the point of stifling their feelings (p. 34). They want to prove us right by love or fear, so they repress their suffering and praise us at the risk of imitating our behavior (pp. 39–42).

**Well-raised children are calm and quiet.**

FALSE. Children who don't talk are not doing well. Indeed, either they are protecting us because they deem us too weak to deal with their problems, or they are afraid of us, and they don't want to take the risk of sharing with us what is going on in their lives, even— and especially—the serious issues they may be going through (p. 145).

**We only think about our children's well-being.**

FALSE. If only! We think more about our own parents' well-being (p. 220) than our children's well-being. We often inflict our childhood suffering on our own children as a way to get revenge (p. 43) and alleviate our pain (p. 53).

**Young children's small misconducts are of no consequence.**

FALSE. To properly judge the behavior of young children, we must picture them acting the same way once they are adolescents or adults and discipline them accordingly (pp. 150–152).

**There's no point in blaming our parents.**

FALSE. There's no point in saying it to their faces, but it's crucial to do an inventory of their strengths and weaknesses, and clearly establish what they did that made us suffer, so that we don't reproduce the same mistakes with our children (pp. 34–43, 61–72).

### We should not give in to our children.

**TRUE and FALSE.** Our children's desires are legitimate. We should thus respond positively to, say, 75 percent of their requests, to show them that their ideas are valid. Such a positive approach gives our children a good image of themselves, and helps them form the habit of expressing their requests accurately (p. 158). However, the fact that our children's desires are legitimate doesn't mean we should always yield to them (p. 160), especially since responding positively does not mean responding immediately. Nevertheless, considering our children's demands as rightful ensures the quality of our relationship with them (p. 178).

### The birth of a child should lead to a fair division of tasks in a household.

**FALSE.** A strict fifty-fifty division of all our parental tasks is an unreasonable expectation, especially if such was not the case with domestic responsibilities before the child's birth, and one partner had already established his or her chores. The involvement of each parent often takes different forms. So if it is reasonable to ask the other for help raising our children, each parent should be able to choose the role he or she will play according to aptitudes and personality. Tasks ought to be assigned to the person best suited to take them on (p. 114).

**When we have children, we don't have any more me time.**

TRUE. But are our children really the only ones taking up all of our time? It's also true of our friendships, our love life, and our work. Life takes time. So why blame this on the children? In reality, this feeling is often due to pressure at work or tensions within our relationship with our partner, which have nothing to do with our children. We prefer placing the blame on them because it's a lot easier and a lot less risky than pointing the finger at our spouse or our coworkers. So it's our children who take the blame (pp. 115–117).

**Having children makes us uncool.**

FALSE. Raising children, far from being boring or conventional, is a life project essential to humankind. It is similar to playing a sport at a professional level, since it requires years of effort before reaching the desired result, and it implies dedication and self-transcendence that bring us, as all adventures do, the greatest possible satisfactions, far superior to having fun going to the movies, for example (p. 109).

**It is exhausting to take care of children.**

TRUE and FALSE. It may be exhausting to care of children, but that is true of any pleasure, including sports or travel, which are activities as tiring as they are rewarding. This feeling of exhaustion thus often stems from our inability to feel pleasure in our children's company. But this pleasure can be learned. Moreover, we need to use precaution with the word "exhaustion" since we tend to turn it into reality. Is it really exhaustion we are feeling? Physical exhaustion is amplified by anxiety. Therefore, most of the time it's the anxiety, not the physical exhaustion, that tires us (p. 117).

### For our children to feel loved, we must tell them we love them.

TRUE and FALSE. More importantly, we need to prove it to them. Otherwise, our children will not feel it. We thus must devote time to them (pp. 122–125), expend energy in order to be "fully present" when we are in their company (p. 137), and take interest in them, especially by addressing their needs (p. 139).

### We must emphasize the quality over the quantity of time we spend with our children.

TRUE and FALSE. We should devote enough time to our children for them to feel important (p. 122). But we must also prioritize them in our schedule whenever possible (p. 124) as well as give them clear and regular blocks of time (p. 125).

### Good old-fashioned methods like "the carrot and the stick" do work.

FALSE. Disciplinarian methods may very well appear effective in the short term, but they push children to lie and conceal, thus altering their ability to feel and to act according to their internal compass. In the long term especially, it leads to the opposite of the desired effect.

Extreme strictness pushes children to obey us by conforming to the image that we have of them, and that justifies our severity and distrust toward them, and also pushes our children to become or to do exactly what we fear most, for example to be lazy, deceitful, and cunning (pp. 144–149).

### We must teach our children to "toughen up" to build their character.

**FALSE.** The idea behind this claim is that if we pay too much attention to our children, they will become "wimps" or "sissies." Yet it's precisely the opposite. If we don't destroy their inner signals, our children get into the habit of paying attention to their symptoms and taking care of themselves, unlike those who have been taught to stoically ignore their feelings and sensations and are not allowed to complain, and who often end up acting irresponsibly and creating their own problems (p. 148).

### Being too permissive is nicer than being too strict.

**FALSE.** At first, being permissive seems both kinder and less harmful to our children than being disciplinarian because our conduct comes from our desire to be loved by them or from our fear of clashing with them. The sources of such lenient behavior strike many, at best, as understandable, and at worse, forgivable acts of cowardice. But being permissive nevertheless falls under the category of abuse because it amounts to us not providing our children with the emotional structure that they need to feel reassured and develop well as people. This authentic negligence triggers anxiety and a feeling of abandonment that often lead children to delinquent or self-destructive behavior (p. 150).

## We shouldn't put up with our children's capricious behavior.

**TRUE and FALSE.** We should not accept that our children throw tantrums in order to get what they want. However, they probably wouldn't do so if we acknowledged their requests and responded to their desires as seriously as we do our own, instead of dismissing their wants as just whims. Indeed, what is the root cause for their capricious behavior, if not the fact that we unfairly deem their genuine desires inappropriate, outrageous, or unjustified? Therefore, rather than dismissing our children's requests on the grounds that they are asking for something that is annoying or inconvenient to us, we ought to acknowledge and respond to their desires as seriously as we do our own, whether favorably or not (p. 152).

## Children are spoiled.

**Often TRUE, but not the way it is ordinarily seen and understood.** To spoil literally means to damage, and there are many ways in which we could spoil our children. Burying them under a pile of gifts is one way, since our apparent generosity that satisfies our joy of giving end ups stifling our children's desire. Therefore, it deprives them of one of their drives in life. But giving nothing to our children, whether by principle or sadism, paradoxically spoils and damages them as well, similarly by extinguishing their desire. Indeed, knowing that their wishes have no chance of being heard or fulfilled, our children will turn to the only recourse available in order to not suffer from that deprivation, which is to switch off their desire altogether (p. 155). But that's not all. Children who are overpraised (p. 68) or on whom we project a flattering image that valorizes them, are also spoiled children, that is to say, abused children (p. 215).

### Responsible and reassuring parents are those who show constant authority in all areas of their children's life.

**TRUE and FALSE.** While parents should be responsible for being vigilant and punishing our children when they stray from our values—even on seemingly minor issues (pp. 150–152)—we have to pick our battles (p. 164) so as not to squander our authority on minor topics such as meals, bedtime, chores, fights between siblings, or during challenging times such as adolescence (pp. 164–175).

### We must give our children self-confidence.

**FALSE.** We don't have the power to do so, and encouraging them artificially does not give rise to assurance, but to conceit, by making our children swing between an inferiority and superiority complex. Only by letting our children overcome their challenges on their own can we convey our trust in their abilities, which then allows them to gain self-confidence (pp. 200–202).

*We make our children's happiness.*

**FALSE.** Again, we do not have this power. Our children must achieve this on their own by overcoming challenges on their own (p. 203). Nevertheless, if we bond with our children by giving them our time and attention, we most often enable them to achieve this (p. 176).

*We should push our children to become independent as soon as possible.*

**FALSE.** The kind of independence that we call for often serves as an excuse to abandon our children. This independence is of no use to them, especially when they are young, because they don't have yet the emotional maturity to cope alone. That is why pushing our children to obtain independence too soon amounts to inflicting mental suffering on them (pp. 207–211). True independence is the one that our children ask for themselves, especially during adolescence. But even though it is anticipated and wished for, we often dread children's independence because it inevitably plunges us into stress and anxiety (p. 174).

*For children to become helpful and obliging adults, they must get in the habit of helping us from a young age.*

**Totally FALSE.** Nothing could be further from the truth. In fact, the opposite is the case. Children can only give what they themselves have received. So we need to be generous with our children and understand that they need to be selfish at home, because they need time and peace of mind without being reprimanded, let alone mistreated, in order to develop as persons. From the time of their infancy until they are about twenty years old, we should take into account our children's needs and desires rather than our own (pp. 129–131), even if what we want is to shower them with kisses, a wish that is ultimately only about pleasing ourselves.

**We must protect our children by sparing them suffering.**

FALSE. We must let our children experience the consequences of their actions (p. 204), which means we have to let them feel pain (p. 202), all while expressing to them the legitimate high expectations that we have for them by demanding they be proud of themselves (p. 218).

**We always know what's best for our children.**

FALSE. This assumption is especially false during our children's adolescence. We believe we have the necessary experience and are well-intentioned enough to interfere in our children's lives, but we are not the greatest judges of what suits them best. Indeed, it's up to our children to "shape" us, and not up to us to "shape" our children, much like teachers, not the other way around (pp. 211–215).

**There is no such thing as a perfect parent.**

TRUE. The good news is that the perfect parent is imperfect. In fact there is no such thing as a perfect parent (pp. 91–94). Furthermore, being aware of our imperfection should make us understand that we are not in the best position to know what is best for our children and to weigh in on their choices whether it comes to school, their relationships, or their professional life. And this should lead us not to interfere in their lives (pp. 212, 217).

### Parents who don't get along should stay together for the good of their children.

**FALSE.** Indeed, it is crucial for children to bring pleasure to their parents since they draw from it their self-confidence. The opposite is also true. In other words, children get the impression that they are worthless if they feel they could be a source of stress, fatigue, and boredom to us, which is inevitably the case if we keep from getting divorced only "for" them, which amounts to making them responsible for our misery. This has harmful and lasting negative consequences for children, who then feel toxic (p. 98).

### We must present a united front to our children.

**FALSE.** Seeing us interact when we disagree with our partner teaches our children how to deal with someone with a different opinion than theirs and how to defend their own ideas when necessary (p. 190). In addition, in cases where we consider that the other parent or caregiver is mistreating our children, it is vital to say so and take an open stand against the offending behavior in our children's presence so that they feel appropriately protected (p. 195).

*Small children, small problems. Big children, big problems.*

**TRUE and FALSE.** True, because as much as it is easy to raise children when they are five years old— teaching them respect and values by correcting their silly, small mistakes on a daily basis—it is much more difficult to start doing so when they are teenagers and their mistakes could lead them to drugs, theft, or self-mutilation (p. 101). But that doesn't mean we should inevitably expect the disasters to increase, especially since small children's suffering can be as important as that of older children, but the only difference is their way of expressing it. The vulnerability and dependence inherent to early childhood often prevent our children from expressing suffering at a young age, and make it more difficult for us to see its subtle signs; but children will make up for this inability later, starting in adolescence, by causing problems through various aggressive behaviors directed at themselves or others (p. 174).

*We have to side with our children's schools and teachers to present to them a coherent wall of authority.*

**FALSE.** We don't need to approve of all of the school's rules or practices to help our children understand that they must follow them if they want to succeed (p. 181). But we have to demonstrate our loyalty to our children by acting as lawyers, advising and protecting them, pleading their case to the school if they are unfairly accused, or demanding amends for any injustice they have suffered, all the while staying by them without excusing or overwhelming them when they do something wrong (p. 196).

### We have a duty to advise our children.

**TRUE and FALSE.** We have the duty to advise and protect our children like lawyers (p. 198), and to help them succeed by setting high expectations. However, we need to be very careful not to confuse being demanding with being intrusive (pp. 211–212). Giving them unsolicited advice is the same as weighing in on their choices and thus forcing their hand (pp. 213–214).

### Adult children have obligations toward their parents.

**FALSE, if we parents are healthy and autonomous.** We often use family obligations as a means to force our adult children to visit us, even if we should (in this order) rejoice that our children no longer need us, try to be interesting so they want to talk to us, and strive to come up with fun and friendly family rituals so that they are drawn to our home (pp. 221–222).

# 3

# Dos

## TAKING CARE OF OUR CHILDHOOD

### 1. *Become aware of the grip our childhood has on us*

- By understanding that we are not freed from our childhood just because we are adults (p. 23).
- By doubting our instinct, in the event we did not have a happy childhood, since it's made of nothing other than our unconscious automatic reflexes inherited from our past, which leads us to reproduce our parents' behavior, and is therefore misleading (pp. 26–33).
- By constantly keeping in mind this repetition mechanism that pushes us to replay our childhood, rather than dismissing it, in order to fight it on a daily basis, and ultimately succeed and overcome it (p. 34).

### 2. *Reevaluate our childhood in order to neutralize it and to transmit only the positive to our children.*

- By allowing ourselves to pass judgment on our parents, without necessarily confronting them (pp. 36–39).
- By reevaluating our childhood with the help of our adult experiences and emotions, in order to understand and validate our past feelings of suffering (p. 61).

- By saying the words that we would have wanted to hear from our own parents while growing up, or by imagining the behavior they should have adopted then, in order to symbolically correct their mistakes after the fact, which will allow us to heal our wounds, and thus move on from the past (p. 73).

### 3. *Correct our behavior as parents*
- By forcing ourselves to be vigilant, asking ourselves: "Is this good for me or for my children?" and, "Is it me, or the echo of my parents that dictates my conduct?" (p. 83).
- By being wary of categorical sentences such as "It's for your own good," or "What makes you think you deserve it?" or "Because I love you," which often serve to legitimize our most shameful unconscious feelings (p. 80).
- By examining, as soon as we become aware of it, any of our behavior that is detrimental to our children, and determining if it stems from our childhood (p. 81). And by keeping in mind that there are multiple ways to duplicate our parents' mistakes (p. 83).
- By finding alternative ways to react (p. 86), not by doing the opposite but by behaving differently and better than our parents (pp. 53–60). This is the only real and rightful way for us to take revenge on our childhood, unlike directing our anger toward our children (pp. 43–48). And by persevering at implementing those better responses despite how difficult it may be, because this process requires perseverance (pp. 84–86).
- By apologizing to our children for our negative responses as soon as we become aware of them, while

we are working at ways to change our behavior. Alternatively, if we only become became aware of these mistakes much later, and our relationship with our children suffers as a result because we hurt them, by acknowledging these mistakes and apologizing to our children. Indeed, children are by nature loving and indulgent toward their parents; therefore, it is never too late to pacify and improve our relationship with them (pp. 36, 221).

## TAKING CARE OF OUR CHILDREN

This means for us to engage fully in our children's upbringing by bonding with them in order to teach them our values, while also allowing them to blossom and develop their own character and strengths until they are ready to go off on their own (p. 22).

1. *Engage fully in our children's upbringing*
- By prioritizing our children (p. 99) without using them an excuse (p. 113). Children draw on our behavior (p. 3). The more attention and love children receive, the more they will thrive; the less they are given, the more they will suffer, and the more they will cause or encounter problems growing up and into adulthood (p. 102).
- By making our children feel important, by clearly making them a priority in our lives. This means actually devoting to them clear and regular blocks of time (p. 125), allocating time for them in our schedule as soon as we

are able to do so (p. 124), and being "fully present" when we are in their company (p. 137).

- By learning to enjoy our children's company because the pleasure we feel with our children gives them the feeling of being precious, and thus valuable. By the same token, they will have the sensation of being worthless if they feel they cause us any stress, fatigue, or boredom (p. 95). Enjoying being with our children requires, among other things, putting aside our fatigue and reflecting on what we do or don't like to do with them and sharing chores and responsibilities with our partner or helping hands, according to personalities and aptitudes (pp. 109–118). But enjoying our children's company also involves sharing our concerns and experiences with other parents to learn from one another. Although this kind of exchange won't actually diminish our load, it changes the way we experience parenting (p. 117).

- By being attentive to our children's well-being. This includes being ruthless in selecting all the helping hands that interact with them—babysitters, music or PE teachers—since we should ensure that we would approve of everything our children might experience in their company. These helping hands have to be able to make up for our shortcomings, such as possessing skills we lack (sports, creative hobbies, etc.) (p. 131).

## 2. *Bond with our children*

- By adopting a positive approach. This means favoring words of encouragement to our children such as,

"I know you can do it" and protecting them from all negative comments (p. 20).

- By taking an interest in them, which means paying attention not only to their health or grades, but also to their friends, the games they play, the movies they like, listening to what they say and reading the books they recommend (p. 138).

- By responding favorably to their requests as often as possible in order to legitimize their desires (p. 158). But without walking away from the rules that we have imposed, because under no circumstances can we allow our children to run wild (p. 157). However, if we refuse our children's requests, it is essential for us to explain our reasoning to them since dismissing our children's wants as just whims only leads them to throw tantrums. Acknowledging their requests and responding to their desires as seriously as we do our own, whether favorably or not, has nothing to do with being permissive (p. 153).

- By bonding with our children, establishing an authentic relationship, which means being honest and up front with our children, for example, regarding our personal needs when we want peace and quiet, by owning up to those needs without pretending it is for the children's own good (pp. 119–120, 169).

- By informing our children of our adult problems and emotions as clearly and simply as possible, so they may be reassured they are right about what they perceive in our lives. They need this confirmation of what they are sensing in order to be set at ease and be able to turn their attention instead to other things that directly interest them (pp. 178–179). It is indeed a mistake to think we are protecting our children by hiding things from them. On the contrary, our children feel guilty and responsible for any problem they perceive to be hanging over us. We are better off expressing our feelings and informing our children in plain language about any major problems of ours so that they understand they are responsible neither for the problem itself nor for coming up with a solution. Otherwise, they will concoct various scenarios to explain our silence or the fact our official story is not consistent with what they sense (pp. 11, 38). Therefore, it is equally unwise to conceal the differences of opinion we have with our partner so as to present our children with a united front, especially since seeing us interact when we disagree teaches our children how to deal with someone with a different opinion than theirs and how to defend their own ideas when necessary (p. 195).

- By discussing all subjects with our children, even those that may not seem child appropriate or to be any of their business (p. 187). Apart from our sex life, which must remain taboo, there is no subject off-limits to children (p. 178). Indeed, happy, healthy children relentlessly ask questions, to which we must answer truthfully, and on all subjects, provided we tailor our comments to their age and abilities. This dialogue should lead our children and us to take turns and share our points of view, since this will teach our children how to think and sharpen their arguments (p. 139).

- By providing them with the keys to connecting with others. This means talking with our children on a daily basis in order for them to understand the people they come across regularly and telling them the realities of the world (pp. 187–189).
- By advising and defending them like a lawyer, in their relationships with their peers as well as with institutions or their other parent. Indeed, our children need from us unconditional benevolence, so we have to prove it to them, daily, by standing by them regardless of the situation, without excusing or overwhelming them when they do something wrong (p. 192). This also means teaching them how to defend themselves (p. 193).

### 3. *Transmit our values*

- By teaching them our values little by little, making use of ordinary circumstances as they come up, to explain, comment, and illustrate our positions to our children (p. 186). It is indeed our duty to transform the society of tomorrow by teaching our children to care for others, and by transmitting to them the values of work, effort, and civic duty, which are all sorely needed in today's difficult world. However, to communicate these values to our child, we need to respect these values ourselves (p. 183).
- By reprimanding our children as soon as their behavior becomes a problem. Often, just telling them to stop is enough to make them do so because our children are so pragmatic they will give up a behavior from which they don't benefit (p. 162). But the sooner we correct

our children's mistakes, the better, since if it is easy
to raise five-year-old children—teaching them respect
and values by correcting their silly, small mistakes on
a daily basis—it is difficult to start to discipline them
when they are teenagers (p. 101). However, to properly
judge our children's behavior, we should imagine that
same behavior carried out by an adolescent or an adult.
If we were to find unacceptable the same conduct in an
older person, we can conclude it would be wrong to let
our children continue behaving in such ways and we
should discipline them accordingly (p. 151).

- By establishing clear, immutable no-nos, that our children can comprehend and respect, and that we enforce
in a calm and confident manner that warrants no backing up or opting out. These nonnegotiables should be
determined based on what is in our children's best interest, in order to prevent them from harming themselves
or others—physically as well as psychologically—so
they can become decent people appreciated by those
around them (p. 152).

- By resorting to sanctions when necessary, provided they
are wisely designed to avoid humiliating or dominating
our children and are proportional to their offense, so
they realize the consequences of their actions (p. 157).

- By picking our battles. Our authority, which isn't
anything else than what our children bestow on us—
whether it is skill, wisdom, knowledge, or experience—
is a precious commodity that we should use sparingly
(p. 164) without squandering it on minor matters
(pp. 167–174).

4. *Let our children develop their own personality and strengths*

- By being attentive to our children's emotions and feelings in order to teach them to trust their own judgment and feelings, which they'll need to rely on like a compass to navigate through their lives. Their desires forge their vitality, much like their emotions and feelings shape their inner compass, which is essential to their mental health and judgment (pp. 19, 47).

- By giving up being overly supportive, thinking it's our responsibility to infuse our children with happiness and self-confidence, and believing that we will achieve this through love and benevolence. Since our continuous waves of encouragement and praise, for no tangible reason, far from boosting our children's self-esteem will inevitably be countered by the merciless responses of the outside world. This contradiction only leads our children to question us and to be confused, which brings them to oscillate between an inferiority and superiority complex. Therefore, our role as parents should be limited to helping them overcome challenges on their own, by being there for them through the good and the bad (p. 200).

- By letting them find their own way and experience the consequences of their actions in order to teach them about responsibility. They must understand they are the one shaping their future, and that their actions are thus their problem (pp. 204–205).

- By accepting their screw-ups, which proves both more challenging and educational than fixing their mistakes (pp. 204, 220).

- By refraining from interfering in their lives and influencing their choices, even if we feel that we have the experience and tenderness required to do so (p. 212). Indeed, although the ideas we have for our children may seem to us smart and rational, they can't suit them because they don't correspond to their choices. And we need to let our children find their way. This entails making a conscious effort to let go of the image we have formed of our children as well as the preconceived idea of success we had in mind for them and backing off and chilling out in order to accept that they will make mistakes (pp. 212–221).

- By setting high expectations. Indeed, it is our duty to give our children the means to fulfill their ambitions and therefore help them succeed. Yet, the only way for us to express the legitimate high expectations we have for them without interfering in their lives or weighing on their decisions is to demand they be proud of themselves (pp. 218–219).

- By rejoicing not to be number one on our adult children's priority list, and by finding a new balance allowing us to continue our relationship with them by being present and available without hanging over their adult lives (p. 221).

4

⤝

# Don'ts

## DO TOO LITTLE

- By not bonding with our children. Indeed, our children develop as individuals through their exchanges with us. Therefore, we, as parents, have a real duty to form a bond with them (pp. 95, 176–191).
- By giving up on experiencing pleasure in our children's company thinking that what really matters is how much time we spend with them, the number of activities we do, and how much we do (p. 134).
- By ignoring our children's feelings, which causes them to dismiss them themselves, and later prevents them from developing the inner compass essential to their mental health and judgment (pp. 7–8). It is the same when we ignore their sensations of hunger and satiety for dietary reasons (p. 167), or their feelings of fear or pain in the name of building character (p. 148), or their enmity for the sake of a moralizing view of the world (p. 187).
- By not acknowledging their requests and dismissing them as whims, when in fact they are genuine desires that we unfairly deem inappropriate or unjustified (p. 152).

- By not making our children our number-one priority, and ignoring them to take care of our love, social, or professional life (p. 99). Indeed, by refusing to make any sacrifices and behaving as if we had no children, we raise children who, down the line, behave as if they had no parents—children who suffer, are delinquent, or harm themselves (p. 102). Our negligence has hugely negative consequences for our children since it amounts to telling them that they aren't worthy of our attention. Such a message creates poor self-esteem that will follow them for the rest of their lives, along with an intense feeling of guilt (p. 124). Being fully engaged in our children's upbringing is not just a moral imperative, but a pragmatic one, as it is the only way for us to have peace of mind when they become adults. It is a rational investment, especially since raising children requires an effort that decreases over time (pp. 101–102).

- By overbooking our children with extracurricular activities, which often allows us to justify and minimize a certain way of abandoning our children. Indeed, we should ask ourselves if we have their best interest in mind, or if, for example, we only want to reassure ourselves as educators, or just buy ourselves extra me time. Caring for children doesn't mean overbooking them. In addition, contrary to what we have always been told, it is a lot easier to use our power of suggestion to influence our children by shaping their aptitudes than to listen and respond to the needs they actually express (p. 134).

- By behaving with our children in reaction to our own childhood rather than according to their best interest and well-being. Chances are our behavior will prove inadequate, if not harmful to them, thus triggering in us a sense of guilt that will in turn lead us, once again, to remain focused on ourselves rather than on our children (pp. 49–52).

- By complaining about our children. First, because they have the impression of being worthless if they feel they are a source of stress, fatigue, or boredom for us (p. 98). And second because, instead of criticizing them, we should question our own behavior toward them: our children's behavior reflects ours, because they imitate everything we parents do, or they react to our influence (pp. 13–19).

- By complaining that our children take up all our time, so much so that we no longer have any me time. Life takes time. And we should keep in mind that everything we do with and for the people we love, whether it be our children, our spouse, or friends, is also "me time," since it contributes to our overall happiness and we are the ones who have made those choices (p. 115). And the least we can say is that having children today is a conscious choice we hold dear to our hearts.

- By choosing not to give them any presents, in order not to spoil them, because we paradoxically spoil and damage our children just the same as parents who shower their children with gifts. Indeed, when children become aware that there is no chance their wants will be fulfilled, they do the only thing they know to avoid suffering, that is, shut down their desires so as not to feel them anymore (p. 155).

- By using our children as an excuse to allow ourselves to behave in ways we don't take responsibility for, as a reason to live, or to save a dying relationship, which only survives or gets better at the expense of our "problem child" (p. 113).

- By giving up disciplining our children and being too permissive, which has nothing to do with being gentle or kind. Permissiveness only amounts to depriving children of the emotional structure that they need to feel safe and develop well. This lenient behavior generates anxiety and a sense of abandonment that often drives children to act up, and may little by little lead them toward delinquency or self-destruction. This is why it is absolutely necessary to correct children when they misbehave, are impolite, pretentious, disdainful, cruel, inconsiderate, or disrespectful toward others (p. 150).

- By not questioning our reactions. We often see our behavior as parents as rational and legitimate, but it is only because it echoes the behavior of our own parents, not because it's actually good for our children. It is therefore imperative to question our conduct by asking if it is effective, positive, and in accordance with our goals as parents, with the help of questions such as "Is my behavior good for me or for my children?" (pp. 82–83).

- By not being up front with our children (p. 120). Being up front with our children only has upsides. Indeed by doing so, we raise them to understand the realities of life. In explaining situations to them frankly, we prove that we value them. Moreover our children are proud to be considered valid interlocutors and to be able to ease our worries. Last but not least, being up front usually leads to good parenting.

- By not being fully present when we are with our children (p. 137). If we allow ourselves to feel tired or distracted, we ultimately won't be able to enjoy the time spent with our children, and they won't be able to be fulfilled either. The same if we talk to them in an absent and distracted manner, or if we run around doing several things at once, since our children become as frustrated as if we had left them all by themselves.

## DO TOO MUCH

- By making children our sole focus, thus neglecting other aspects of our lives, whether they be emotional, professional, or cultural. Doing so burdens children with the overwhelming feeling of being entirely responsible for our well-being, which is terribly distressing. And in the end, making children our sole focus leads us to make them the cause of the frustration we inevitably feel when we make those sacrifices, which has disastrous consequences for them (p. 112).
- By overdoing it with child supervision. Most American parents believe children must be protected and accompanied at all times, but professionals are beginning to point to research indicating that this helicopter-parenting attitude leads children to be anxious and depressed, and diminishes or even precludes resilience (pp. 127–129).

- By wanting to be infallible. First, because it would be overbearing for our children to have perfect parents. And if we were, they would never be able to leave us (p. 221). Second, because being wrong gives us the opportunity to acknowledge our mistakes by going back on our words or actions, and to give our children a practical lesson in honesty (p. 180).
- By believing we need to control our children by interfering in their lives. It is essential that, while being present and supportive, we also keep our distance (p. 212). Demanding that our children conform to the image we have of them when we see fit is likely to crush their inner rhythm or personality (p. 215). It may also lead them to give up their own personality altogether. Indeed, this controlling behavior suggests to them that we are not interested in them, but in their image, which leaves them with no other choice but to follow our implicit orders so they are not ignored or rejected (pp. 59, 217).
- By being too strict, which proves to be a counterproductive parenting method, since it has disastrous effects on children. In the short term, if children obey our orders thanks to violent and humiliating tactics that establish a relationship that is based on fear and animosity, then in the long term, they will also obey the negative image we have of them. This likely will lead to children becoming or doing exactly what we fear most (p. 144). Moreover, being too strict pushes our children to please or oppose us because we wield the carrot and the stick, rather than learn to trust their own judgment

and feelings, which they need to rely on like a compass to navigate through their lives (p. 145).

- By playing young and cool or buddy-buddy with our children, which in reality is an insidious way of dominating them by imposing on them a complicity that they don't want in the first place (p. 70). Stealing our children's thunder as cool teenagers prevents them from dissociating from us parents and by extension from becoming adults. Although seemingly harmless and even fun, these types of parent-buddy relationships push teenagers to want to distinguish themselves from our generation by outdoing our own transgressions (pp. 71, 175).

- By expressing our fears and exclaiming, for example, "You're going to fall!" or "I'm really afraid you're failing at school." Such expressions are taken as orders to fall or fail, since children don't perceive the meaning of words as much as the emotions behind them, and they interpret negative emotions as orders to fail, and positive ones as encouragements to succeed (p. 16). Instead, we should do our best to get a handle on our anxiety, which, although inevitable, is harmful to our children (p. 19). And this all the more since we often believe that our concern justifies our intrusiveness, even though we should actually let go of the control we have over our children so they may gain independence (pp. 198, 207).

- By rushing to fulfill our children's demands as if it were an emergency, which suggests they are in some kind of danger, and fosters a feeling of anxiety in them as well as in us, whereas frustration—in small doses—has educational value because it acclimates our children to the idea that they might not always get what they want, or at least not right away and that they are perfectly capable of handling it (p. 160).

- By preventing our children from doing things for themselves. Indeed, overcoming challenges on their own is so beneficial to children that it is essential that we refrain as early as possible from interfering in their lives in order to spare them from hardships and hurdles. Otherwise, it sends them the message that we believe they are not capable of overcoming difficulty on their own (p. 202).

- By showering our children with gifts. Our apparent generosity, while satisfying our joy of giving, stifles our children's wants and desires and deprives them of one of their drives in life. This is not the case when presents stand as rewards, since the efforts made by our children to deserve these presents give them the opportunity to overcome difficulties, and thus succeed. The pleasure they get from these actual gifts is therefore doubled by the pleasure and pride they get from their achievements (p. 155).

- By trying to instill in our children happiness and self-confidence, and believing that we will achieve this through love and benevolence (p. 200). Our continuous waves of encouragement and praise, given for no tangible reason, far from boosting our children's self-esteem, will inevitably be countered by the merciless responses of the outside world. This contradiction only leads our children to question us and to be confused, which brings them to oscillate between an inferiority and superiority complex. Therefore, our role as parents should be limited to helping them overcome challenges on their own by being there for them through the good and the bad (p. 203).

- By getting involved in our children's relationships with each other, because it tends to create jealousy among them, which is neither automatic nor inevitable. Also, when we do get involved, we often don't understand the situation we've stepped into in order to end disputes between our children. We may very well, for example, accuse the wrong child and punish the eldest when in reality the youngest is the one who caused trouble. This then discredits our authority and fosters resentment among siblings (p. 171).

- By believing we should show constant authority in all areas of our children's lives. If we are responsible for being vigilant and punishing our children when they stray from our values—even on seemingly minor issues (p. 151)—we have to pick our battles (p. 164) so as not to squander our authority on minor topics such as meals, bedtime, chores, fights between siblings, or during challenging times such as adolescence (pp. 167–174).

- By believing it's our job as parents to control our children's development and to decide on how and when to grant them independence. The kind of independence that we call for often serves as an excuse to abandon our children. This independence is of no use to them, especially when they are young, because they don't yet have the emotional maturity to cope alone. That is why pushing our children to obtain independence too soon amounts to inflicting mental suffering on them (p. 130). True independence is the kind that children ask for themselves, especially during adolescence. But even though it is anticipated and wished for, we often dread children's independence because it inevitably plunges us into stress and anxiety (pp. 129, 207).

- By believing we should control how and when to grant independence to our children. Independence is something all children aspire to, and something we need to support by letting them determine how they want to achieve it. Also, we ought to content ourselves with just being at our children's side throughout their upbringing, at first physically and later symbolically, to make them feel safe and allow them to reach this goal (p. 202). We should therefore grant them the independence they ask for, especially when they are teenagers. Indeed, the infamous "adolescent crisis" often has less to do with children, who have every right to emancipate themselves, than with us parents, who struggle so much to relinquish our control that we impose onto them irrational and sometimes even unjust rules (p. 203). Furthermore, we should keep in mind that we would be taking greater risks by not giving our children their independence, since we would then forever suffer from the consequences of their lack of independence (p. 207).

- By influencing our children's choices because it's up to them to "shape" us as parents, and not the other way around. We should realize that taking control of our children's lives by saying "Do this" or "Do that" in order for them to conform to our expectations is no different than trampling them. Not to mention we may use inappropriate or outdated reasoning, and our errors in judgment could have serious consequences for our children (pp. 212–218).

# Notes

1   John Bowlby, *Le lien, la psychanalyse et l'art d'être parent*, trans.
    Yvane Wiart (Paris: Albin Michel, 2011), 43–51; 183–187.
    Jacques Dayan, "Le bébé des neurosciences," *Spirale*, no. 76
    (2015): 18–23.

2   Blaise Pierrehumbert, *Le Premier lien: Théorie de l'attachement*
    (Paris: Odile Jacob, 2003), 46–50.

3   John Bowlby, *Maternal Care and Mental Health: A Report
    Prepared on Behalf of the World Health Organization as a
    Contribution to the United Nations Programme for the Welfare of
    Homeless Children* (Geneva: World Health Organization, 1951),
    11–12.

4   Ibid., 16–17.

5   Salomon Sellam, *L'incorporation émotionnelle: aimer à en tomber
    malade* (Montreuil-Bonnin: Bérangel Editions, 2014), 41.

6   Joëlle Rochette-Guglielmi, "Le bébé agent des états mentaux
    d'autrui," *Spirale*, no. 76 (2014–5): 77–85.

7   Georges Menahem, "Troubles de santé à l'âge adulte et
    difficultés familiales dans l'enfance," *Persée* 47, no. 4 (1992):
    893–932; Eric Albert and Laurent Chneiweiss, *L'Anxièté
    au quotidien* (Paris: Éditions Odile Jacob, 1990); Sellam,
    *L'incorporation émotionnelle*, 45–47. See also https://www
    .ncbi.nlm.nih.gov/pubmed/25025476 and http://www

.theasthmacenter.org/index.php/faq/is_asthma_an_emotional_disease/

8   M. Krebs, "Troubles psychiatriques, génétique ou environnement: vers la fin du débat?," *L'information psychiatrique* 83, no. 2 (2007), 117–121; J.-C. Poncer and B. Chamak, "Génétique des troubles psychiatriques," *La lettre des Neurosciences: Bulletin de la Société des Neurosciences* no. 29 (2005), 7–11.

9   Cindy Hazan and Phillip Shaver, "Romantic Love Conceptualized as an Attachment Process," *Journal of Personality and Social Psychology* 52, (1987): 511–24; and Phillip Shaver, Cindy Hazan, and Donna Bradshaw, "Love as Attachment: The Integration of Three Behavioral Systems" in *The Psychology of Love*, ed. R.J. Sternberg and M.L. Barnes (New Haven, CT: Yale University Press, 1988), 68–99.

10  Lenore Skenazy, *Free-Range Kids: How to Raise Safe, Self-Reliant Children (Without Going Nuts with Worry)* (San Francisco: Jossey-Bass, 2010). See also https://www.theatlantic.com/magazine/archive/2014/04/hey-parents-leave-those-kids-alone/358631/

11  Peter Gray, "Declining Student Resilience: A Serious Problem for Colleges," *Psychology Today* (March 22, 2015): https://www.psychologytoday.com/us/blog/freedom-learn/201509/declining-student-resilience-serious-problem-colleges

12  Deena Prichep, "To Raise Confident, Independent Kids, Some Parents Are Trying to 'Let Grow,'" *Morning Edition*, NPR, September 3, 2018, https://www.npr.org/sections/health-shots/2018/09/03/641256596/to-raise-confident-independent-kids-some-parents-are-trying-to-let-grow

13  Sellam, *L'incorporation émotionelle*, 41; and Laurent Daillie, *La Logique du symptôme* (Montreuil-Bonnin: Bérangel, 2006).